T0339415

Age Friendly

"Age Friendly provides a clear roadmap detailing how we can and should make ageism a thing of the past. Samuel flips ageism on its head by showing that our aging population is an asset rather than a liability."

Ken Dychtwald, PhD,
best-selling author of 18 books, including
What Retirees Want and Radical Curiosity

"As longevity gets longer, age isn't what it used to be. Larry Samuel is one of the most persuasive advocates for a positive re-set of how our culture treats age."

Peter Hubbell,
Founder & CEO, BoomAgers

"Comprehensive, intriguing, and offering many solutions. A proclamation giving us permission to rid ourselves of ageism now."

Sharon Rose, M.S.,
social gerontologist

Age Friendly
Ending Ageism in America

Lawrence R. Samuel

Routledge
Taylor & Francis Group

A PRODUCTIVITY PRESS BOOK

First published 2022
by Routledge
600 Broken Sound Parkway #300, Boca Raton FL, 33487

and by Routledge
2 Park Square, Milton Park, Abingdon, Oxon, OX14 4RN

Routledge is an imprint of the Taylor & Francis Group, an informa business

Library of Congress Cataloging-in-Publication Data
A catalog record for this book has been requested

ISBN: 978-1-032-05145-1 (hbk)
ISBN: 978-1-032-05144-4 (pbk)
ISBN: 978-1-003-19623-5 (ebk)

DOI: 10.4324/9781003196235

Typeset in Garamond
by Apex CoVantage, LLC

Contents

About the Author vii
Introduction 1

1 Ageism in America... **11**
   How Old Are You? 12
   The Cult of Youth 15
   Aging Is a Privilege.. 18
   The Demographic Cliff 21
   A Vast and Strange Generation.................................. 23
   OK Boomer 26
   Younger Minds.. 29

2 Age-Friendly Communities **35**
   A Silver Tsunami 36
   The Age of Aging 39
   Livability for All.. 43
   Active Senior Living.. 45
   10,000 Americans 47
   It's Not about Leaves 49
   The Place They Call Home.. 51

3 Age-Friendly Work **57**
   I'm Not Done 58
   Yesterday's News.. 60
   Unretirement 62
   Encore Careers 64
   The Value of Experience 66
   Living, Learning, and Earning Longer......................... 67
   Knowledge Transfer... 70
   A New Social Contract.. 72
   Unlock the Potential 74

4 Age-Friendly Marketing 79
    Old Age Is Made Up 80
    No One over 40 83
    Aging Is an Opportunity 86
    A Bogus Image 89
    The Newest Battlefield 91
    Boomers 3.0 95

5 Age-Friendly Responsibility 103
    The Beating Heart 104
    A Responsibility Revolution 107
    A Connected Economy 110
    Growing With Age 113
    Long Overdue 116
    A Rising Wave 119
    An Age-Neutral Workplace 121

6 Conclusion 127

Bibliography 135

Index 139

About the Author

Lawrence R. Samuel is the founder of the Miami- and New York City-based consultancy AmeriCulture and is the author of many books, including *Aging in America* and *Boomers 3.0*. He writes "Psychology Yesterday," "Boomers 3.0," and "Future Trends" blogs for psychologytoday.com and is a regular contributor to "The Age of Aging" blog on MediaVillage.com. Larry holds a Ph.D. in American Studies from the University of Minnesota and was named a 2017 NextAvenue Influencer in Aging. He is a member of the Miami-Dade Age Friendly initiative.

Introduction

I'm a white male of fairly average body size and shape, something that throughout my life has made me immune to the lifelong discrimination often faced by women, people of color, and plus-sizers. Upon entering my 60s, however, I began to confront ageist thinking and practices, a result, no doubt, of my appearance and the graduation dates on my resume, which went back to the 1970s. Being invited to join AARP at age 50 was a bit of a shock, but now I was being asked if I needed help getting groceries to my car and instantly dismissed as a job candidate by an artificial intelligence (AI) robot because of my age.

Given my previous privileged status, this was a rather surprising and disturbing development. "Old age is the most unexpected of all things that happen to a man," mused Leon Trotsky, a sentiment that the Marxist revolutionary and I (oddly) share. Like many people who are marginalized in some way because of how they appear, I decided to try to change people's (mis)perceptions about aging in the pursuit of equality. In short, I'm doing what I can to persuade others to not use an individual's age as a reliable measure to judge her or his worth as a human being. This book is one result of that effort.

While I don't like it a bit, I can understand how in our youth-dominant society the physical signs of older age—gray hair and wrinkles, notably—or birth dates are (mistakenly) equated with decline and irrelevance. A host of myths and stereotypes—e.g., that older people can't learn new things and are just shadows of the active people they used to be—are wrapped up in our deeply rooted ageism that is said to be the only tolerated form of discrimination. Because it is culturally based and built on generations of now outdated thinking, ageism in America admittedly represents a mighty challenge to defeat. Still, it's worth the effort to try, I and thousands of other "pro-aging" activists believe, as millions of people in this country and around the world suffer in some way directly because of it.

The irony of ageism is that the third act of life is actually mostly about the pursuit of wisdom, self-actualization, and leaving some kind of legacy. The distressing changes to one's body that come with aging are often countered by an evolution of mind and spirit, with one's older years typically a period of intellectual growth, accelerated creativity, emotional contentedness, and a desire to take on new challenges. Happily, the attributes that naturally come with age—experience, perspective, judgment, notably—have recently gained considerable value and social currency, as it is these qualities that prove most useful in making decisions and solving problems. Older adults are thus in an ideal position to make valuable contributions to society and, at the same, find personal contentment and a sense of well-being.

The most important thing to know about older adults is that they're not done yet. The "Greatest Generation" survived the Depression and saved the American Way of Life in World War II, but baby boomers (currently in their late 50s to mid-70s) are now reinventing the concept of older age—a historic achievement in itself. For the past century in the United States, the post-employment stage of life was viewed as a kind of epilogue to the main body of work. There were exceptions, of course, but people older than 65 were generally considered no longer active, productive, and contributing members of society. The passage of Social Security in the 1930s and Medicare in the 1960s was of tremendous benefit but made older Americans appear like dependents and further marginalized them from the rest of the "useful" population.

Baby boomers are changing that perception, a cultural pivot point that will perhaps serve as their greatest legacy. Rather than shift into lower gear, many older adults are pursuing their personal and professional passions as vigorously as ever. This is a very good thing, as physical and mental health have been shown to worsen without having some meaning and purpose in life. Whatever it may be, it's critical to have a reason to get up in the morning. Giving back in some way—i.e., enabling the happiness of others—is the best medicine of all, something many boomers are finding.

Pervasive ageism, however, deeply affects the way older adults view themselves and their everyday lives. Prevailing standards of beauty grounded in youthfulness dictate that many, if not most, older people are deemed unattractive, fueling the insidious anti-aging business. We're also believed to be physically and cognitively impaired and that we can no longer do the things that younger people can. With this kind of ageist mind–body punch, is it any wonder that lots of young adults don't want older people around, particularly in the workplace? We all know one can't judge a book by its cover, but that rule doesn't seem to apply with regard to age. I feel and think of myself as essentially the same person I was when I was younger, but this is clearly not the case for pretty much everyone else who encounters me or my fellow sexagenarians.

Despite all this, there are reasons to believe that we can permanently put an end to ageist thinking and practices over the next couple of decades. First of all,

America is an inherently pluralistic nation where discrimination based on age, just like that based on race or gender, has no place. As well, we are currently experiencing a golden age of social activism that rivals that of the counterculture, and what I call age friendliness can surf on the waves being created by the Black Lives Matter and MeToo movements.

The fact that ageism is even a subject worth discussing is surprising given that the aging population is arguably the biggest story of our time and place. There are now more older people in the United States and on the planet than at any other time in history, a seismic shifting of our cultural plates that will accelerate over the next couple of decades. The number of people aged 65+ will grow to one billion in 2030, according to the World Health Organization (WHO); this age group is increasing four times faster than the rest of the population. This "silver tsunami," as some people refer to the rising wave of older adults, is the result of a perfect demographic storm, specifically declining birthrates, increased life expectancy, and the aging of baby boomers.

Given such numbers, I would expect that there would no longer be such a thing as ageism. How could such a large, collectively wealthy, and politically engaged group be the target of virulent discrimination, especially in the workplace? While it makes no sense to me, it is very real, I can personally attest, and it's up to us to try to change things for the better. Baby boomers are in the bullseye of ageism, making it sensible for them to do the heavy lifting in this worthy pursuit. Fortunately, boomers like myself have a long history fighting the "system" in order to make the country live up to its noble ideals, and more of us are signing up every day to take on this important cause.

Age Friendly: Ending Ageism in America is designed to serve as a rallying call for baby boomers and like-minded folks to make the United States a more equitable and just nation in terms of age. Virtually all aspects of everyday life in America will be impacted by the doubling or tripling of the number of older people over the next two decades, more reason to adopt age friendliness as a cause. "Age friendliness" means being inclusive toward older people as workers, consumers, and citizens, something that can't be said to exist today. The United States and, especially, Big Business, are notoriously age-unfriendly places, I argue, a result of our obsession with youth. America and Americans have a major problem when it comes to aging, so much so that it (along with death) remains our last cultural taboo.

This book is designed to be a useful resource for all kinds of readers—general, academic, and practitioners, particularly those within the business community. It shows how large companies are in an ideal position to address the aging of America and, in the process, benefit from making their organizations more age friendly. Because of its economic power and commitment to diversity in the workplace, Big Business—specifically the Fortune 1000—has the opportunity and I believe responsibility to take a leadership role in changing the narrative of aging in America.

At the intersection of two megatrends—aging and diversity—age friendliness appears to be in the right place at the right time. *Age Friendly* attempts to show that age friendliness offers the possibility of bridging the gaps not just between younger and older people but also those based on income, class, race, gender, politics, and geography. Inclusion is at the heart of age friendliness, not just the providing of equal access but also making people feel they are part of something bigger than themselves. More than anything else, this book presents a bold and counterintuitive idea—aging is a positive thing for businesses, individuals, and society as a whole—and we should embrace it rather than fear it.

Not surprisingly, given the richness of the subject and its universality, quite a few other authors have, of course, offered their thoughts on aging and ageism. (This is actually my third contribution to the field, having written a cultural history of aging in America and a guide to marketing to baby boomers in their third act of life.) Robert N. Butler can be said to have pioneered the field with his 1975 *Why Survive? Being Old in America*, which I discuss in the first chapter, but he went further on the topic in his 2008 *The Longevity Revolution: The Benefits and Challenges of Living a Long Life.* Human life expectancy grew slowly over the course of 5,000 years but quickly accelerated in the 20th century, Butler pointed out, a fact whose implications we haven't fully considered. Butler labeled this historic transformation "the longevity revolution" and raised many of the social and economic consequences that have grown out of it. Like myself, however, Butler remained optimistic about our ability to meet the many challenges posed by our living longer lives while conceding that much thought and effort is needed. "We have the tools to take advantage of this exceptional demographic shift," he wrote, "but it will require nothing less than a total transformation of both the personal experience of aging and of cultural attitudes."[1]

In her *Life Gets Better: The Unexpected Pleasures of Growing Older*, Wendy Lustbader, a social worker, flipped aging on its head, positing that most of us have it backward. "The myth of youth as the best time of life burdens the young and makes us all dread getting older, as though there is only diminishment of life's bounty as decades pass," she wrote, thinking that a book that proclaimed the opposite would be well received. That "life gets better" rather than worse as one ages may be hard for most young people to believe but has been well documented by many research studies. Later life was a "source of ever-expanding inner and outer discovery," she heard from many older friends; her book was a loud retort to the stereotypes about aging that can be summed up as one big downer. Instead, self-knowledge, insight, and confidence came with the years, as Lustbader's collection of stories showed, the added plus being that older people didn't care a whole lot about what people thought of them.[2]

Margaret Cruikshank's *Learning to Be Old: Gender, Culture, and Aging*, meanwhile, focused on our denial of aging and how because of that we essentially had to learn how to be old. The physical changes that come with aging take place within a social context, Cruikshank, a feminist scholar, argued, meaning that gender, race, class, and even the economic and political climate played important roles in the process. "Learning to be old requires that we both observe how aging is constructed and find ways to resist being molded to its dictates," she wrote, rejecting the popular notions of "successful aging" and "productive aging." Because women lived longer than men, they especially needed to learn how to be old, making gender central to the subject of aging and ageism.[3]

In *The Upside of Aging: How Long Life Is Changing the World of Health, Work, Innovation, Policy and Purpose*, a collection of essays, editor Paul Irving, president of the Milken Institute, credited baby boomers like himself for bringing about the title of the book. "Many years ago, my generation challenged authority and convention and, in doing so, redefined an age," Irving wrote, "and the baby boomers are at it again, changing expectations and the way we think about aging." While greater longevity presented many challenges on both an individual and societal level, what he considered "possibly the most important development in human history" also offered great opportunities. The key to realizing the full potential of the aging revolution was to discard the tropes of dependency and decline and replace them with the realities of a very different kind of older population. Just about everything—health, work, education, cities, the economy, and much more—will change in the years ahead, Irving and his contributors believed, making us lucky to live in such historically significant times.[4]

In her pithily titled *How to Age*, Anne Karpf made the case that aging is culturally defined but suggested that fear and shame are the principal emotions that we assign to it. That we group people into the bucket of "old" when they reach a certain age—60, 50, and now even 40—is itself an absurd thing, she maintained, with little or no positive social value attached to reaching that biological destination. The commonly perceived loss of individuality that is associated with aging is especially annoying to Karpf, a sociologist and journalist. "We become more, and not less, diverse as we age," she wrote, a result of the experience that we accumulate over the years. Pushing aging to the back end of life is also misdirected, Karpf proposed. "Aging is a lifelong process, not something confined to its latter stages," she pointed out, a realization that would help people face and even look forward to the prospect of getting older.[5]

The big idea of Carl Honore's 2019 *Bolder: Making the Most of Our Longer Lives* was that our custom of dividing a life into three neat parts only contributed to ageist thinking and practices. Why did early life have to be about education, middle life about working, and later life about leisure? Wouldn't it be better to scramble those divisions up to make a more holistic life that offered more possibilities all along the journey? Blurring the traditional boundaries of age would go a long way toward ending the prejudices woven into getting older, Honore, a Canadian journalist, argued, a compelling thesis. Honore not only recommends breaking down generational divisions but also proactively finding ways to get people of different ages together, a theme that I discuss relative to age-friendly communities in Chapter 2 of this book.[6]

Finally, Louise Aronson's *Elderhood: Redefining Aging, Transforming Medicine, Reimagining Life* addressed our health-care system in relation to the aging population. Aronson, a geriatrician, observed much bias built into the ways that older people are treated as patients, something that both reflected and shaped the ways they were viewed in broader society. Aronson took special aim at anti-aging and viewing getting older as a disease, something that also resonates in these pages. "The world offers us so many opportunities to create an old age we need not dread," she wrote, urging her colleagues to make that possible.[7]

Age Friendly makes a similar appeal by detailing how the age-friendly movement can serve as our best chance to realize the kind of upside that these authors imagined. Chapter 1, "Ageism in America," shows how ageism is a pervasive force in America that, like racism and gender discrimination, runs contrary to our democratic ideals. I briefly trace the history of aging in America, showing how older people became increasingly marginalized through the 20th century. I then bring that less than happy story up to today, making the case that ageism is a fact of life for the tens of millions of baby boomers still very much around. (The number that have died is about equal to the number of immigrants to the United States who fall within the generational age range.) Boomer bashing is in vogue these days, a backlash against the once largest generation in history who achieved great things but are now commonly blamed for much of the world's problems.

Ageism is especially apparent in Big Business, I continue in the first chapter of the book. People in their third act of life are generally not welcome as workers, consumers, or citizens in major companies, a by-product of our negative attitudes toward older people. I debunk the many myths surrounding older people and show that such untrue stereotypes are part and parcel of our deeply and culturally rooted ageism. I then describe the generational traits of baby boomers and explain why many Gen Xers and millennials are less than fond of them.

Fortunately, I add, there are things we can and should do to make the country a more age-friendly place, a worthy and long overdue endeavor. We're all aging, after all, making the reality of getting older a universal experience to which each of us can relate. Sending this message to Corporate America—especially the Fortune 1000—represents our biggest opportunity to address the nation's aging problem. For these companies, taking proactive steps to change the narrative of aging in America is not just the right thing to do but also a smart business strategy. It can and should be considered a corporate initiative that will yield bottom-line results for years to come, one that will spark a trickle-down effect across society, including the public sector.

Chapter 2, "Age-Friendly Communities," brings the good news that efforts are being made to end ageism in America and around the world via the age-friendly movement. The WHO is currently leading the movement, focusing its effort on making communities more age friendly. A growing number of cities and towns around the world are striving to better meet the needs of their older residents by joining WHO's Global Network for Age-friendly Cities and Communities. While their efforts to become more age friendly take place within very different cultural, social, and economic settings, all members of the network have the common desire and commitment to improve the quality of life for their older residents. Within the United States, WHO's effort is led by AARP, the country's leading advocate for the aging population. More and more communities across the country are eagerly joining the network, as local leaders recognize both the challenges and the opportunities that older residents present.

Chapter 3, "Age-Friendly Work," discusses the ways in which Corporate America is decidedly age unfriendly. Employees over the age of 50 are often encouraged to take early retirement or simply pushed out the door, seen as both too costly and past their prime. Likewise, anyone with a college degree from the 1970s or even later has a slim chance of getting an interview, much less a job within the managerial ranks of any major company. This is unfortunate (and unethical and illegal), I explain, as an intergenerational workforce would be in the best interest of not just older people but also the companies themselves. Age brings experience, perspective, and wisdom—just the right skill set for both short- and long-term decision-making.

Ageism in the workplace today is reminiscent of the long and ugly history of keeping women and people of color out of Corporate America, I continue in Chapter 3. Much of the ageism at work today has to do with the simple fact that young adults prefer to be around other younger adults in both social settings and on the job. Sadly, millennials (and C-suite boomers, it needs to be said) have taken active steps to perpetuate that situation via ageist hiring and retention policies. The result is that age is the only remaining demographic criterion in which it is acceptable to discriminate, something often justified as "overqualification." In theory, age is often part of a diversity and inclusion initiative, but it is rarely put into practice.

Need it be said, with their gradual retirement of retirement, most baby boomers want to continue working as long as possible. We're living longer lives, for one thing, and money comes in very handy at any age. More than that, however, work is a prime source of identity for individuals and often adds years to longevity. Corporate America should incorporate older people in its commitment to diversity and inclusion, as those companies that do so will be the winners of the economy of the future. Happily, with its "Living, Learning, and Earning Longer" initiative, AARP and its partners the Organisation for Economic Co-operation and Development and the World Economic Forum are doing yeoman's work by encouraging employers to create a multigenerational workforce. Dozens of corporations have enlisted in that initiative, precisely what needs to happen for age friendliness to blossom in the business world.

Chapter 4, "Age-Friendly Marketing," explains how the aging of America presents major implications for businesses in virtually all industries and product categories. Baby boomers are still the key to the marketplace despite marketers' focus on youth, due much in part to their collective wealth and propensity to consume. Boomers' buying power is and will remain huge, more reason why marketers should not think the group's best consumer days are behind them. Much of Chapter 4 has to do with what has been called "the longevity economy," i.e., the billions of dollars that older consumers spend each year and the goldmine that looms in the future as they become an even bigger percentage of the population. I provide some examples of the relatively few marketers who are getting it right and present my own platform for effectively marketing to the boomers.

The final chapter of *Age Friendly*, "Age-Friendly Responsibility" examines corporate social responsibility (CSR), a self-regulating business model that helps a company be socially accountable—to itself, its stakeholders, and the public. CSR refers to practices and policies that are intended to "do good" in the world in some meaningful way. More corporations are pursuing "prosocial" objectives in addition to maximizing profits, a goal that can be synergistic rather than mutually exclusive. Through CSR programs and volunteer efforts, businesses can benefit society while boosting their brands, a win-win scenario. Such activities can also increase employee loyalty and boost morale by making workers and employers feel more connected with the world around them.

Chapter 5 then discusses ways that companies can be good citizens by supporting age friendliness on a local, state, or national level. Donating money, time, or products and services to relevant social causes and nonprofits is just one way this can be done. Participating in community events and encouraging employees to volunteer time to programs dedicated to older adults is something companies should consider, as it not only benefits people who could use some help but is good for business.

There are some very good reasons for America and the rest of the world to be age friendly, I conclude in this book, an idea that I hope resonates with each and every reader.

Notes

1 Robert N. Butler, MD, *The Longevity Revolution: The Benefits and Challenges of Living a Long Life* (New York: Public Affairs, 2008) xi–xii.

2 Wendy Lustbader, *Life Gets Better: The Unexpected Pleasures of Growing Older* (New York: TarcherPerigee, 2011).

3 Margaret Cruikshank, *Learning to Be Old: Gender, Culture, and Aging* (Lanham, MD: Rowman & Littlefield, 2013) 1–3.

4 Paul Irving, *The Upside of Aging: How Long Life Is Changing the World of Health, Work, Innovation, Policy and Purpose* (Hoboken, NJ: Wiley, 2014) xx.

5 Anne Karpf, *How to Age* (New York: Picador, 2015) 1–4.

6 Carl Honore, *Bolder: Making the Most of Our Longer* (Toronto, CA: Knopf, 2018).

7 Louise Aronson, *Elderhood: Redefining Aging, Transforming Medicine, Reimagining Life* (New York: Bloomsbury, 2021) 160.

Chapter 1

Ageism in America

We're all going to get old (if we're lucky).

David Rotman
Editor-at-Large of MIT Technology Review

In December 2018, an age discrimination complaint was filed to the New York Division of Human Rights by one Michael Boyajian. Who had Boyajian accused of infringing upon his rights? The Rolling Stones, of all people, who were all in their 70s at the time. Boyajian, who required a walker to get around after a fall, claimed that the band and their promoter, Concerts West/AEG, were charging five times the normal ticket price for a disabled seat to an upcoming show at MetLife Stadium in East Rutherford, New Jersey. "Baby boomers are their biggest fans, and we're ageing out now," Boyajian explained, thinking the "Strolling Bones," as the four-member band was now sometimes called because of its collective age of 298, was an ageist organization.[1]

The story illustrates how prevalent ageism was and remains in America and much else of the world. As youth culture made a rapid ascent in the late 1960s, "oldness culture" made an equivalent descent in terms of social worth or value. Over the last half-century and change, Americans in their third act of life have been engaged in a cultural war to realize the same civil rights as younger people but, it can be safely argued, they have lost most of the battles. Older Americans can be seen as a minority group but without the legal protections that other groups enjoy, a double whammy of discrimination. A host of factors—the historical legacy of ageism, the popularity of "anti-aging" modalities, persistent myths and stereotypes about older people, a hatred of baby boomers by younger generations, a virulent form of age-based bias in the

DOI: 10.4324/9781003196235-2   11

workplace, and an utter failure by our legal system—have nurtured the ageist climate we have today in this country.

Still, despite all this, there is reason to be hopeful that ageism will wane over the next couple of decades. Millions more Americans are heading into their 70s every year, for one thing, a shifting of our demographic plates that may trigger social, economic, and political progress. Already there seems to be a sea change bubbling up as the fight against the untenable proposition of ageism reaches a critical mass. More baby boomers (who were likely ageist in their younger days, it needs to be said) are rather suddenly realizing they have joined the older crowd and are finding the cause to be one to which they can personally relate. While much has to be done to wipe out or even seriously damage ageist thinking and practices, a strong sense of social activism is currently in the air, making the prospect of an age-friendly America a very real one.

How Old Are You?

Given the deep roots of ageism in this country, we definitely have a long way to go. "Old age in America is often a tragedy," the opening sentence of Robert Butler's *Why Survive? Being Old in America* reads, about as depressing as eight words can be to anyone in their third act of life. The 1975 book is now considered a classic, not only because it won a Pulitzer Prize but due to its blazing of the trail of "ageism" (a term Butler had coined in 1968 when he recognized discrimination of older people). As the founding director of the National Institute on Aging (NIA), Butler was in an ideal position to recognize the marginalized status of the elderly at the time of the nation's bicentennial. (Butler was clearly ahead of his time; as the first chair of a geriatrics department at an American teaching hospital, Mount Sinai in New York City, he made Alzheimer's disease a primary area of research.) Old age conveyed sickness and death, he argued, running directly counter to our cultural values rooted in youthful exuberance and productivity. Even then, most older Americans were reasonably healthy, making the fear and dread associated with aging a social construct versus a reflection of reality. Butler went on in the book to outline how the United States was not just neglectful to its older citizens but often cruel to them. This was a shameful thing given our noble ideals and wealth, he concluded, calling for a wholesale reexamination of public policy to correct the injustice.[2]

In his 1989 *How Old Are You? Age Consciousness in America*, Howard Chudacoff makes a distinction between the biological phenomenon of age and the social meanings we assign to it. An individual's status is heavily defined by their age and, in Western society, one's status tends to become greater in one's 20s and decline in one's 60s. Chudacoff traces what would become to be called ageism to the late 19th century as before that Americans didn't think too much about age. Segmentation in many forms becomes common after that, this divvying up of society working to the disadvantage of those believed to be unable to contribute economically. It wasn't until Robert Butler introduced the idea of ageism into public discourse, however, that the field became canonized. "Since the 1960s, ageism has attracted increasing attention from those concerned with discrimination in American society," Chudakoff wrote, the parallels to be drawn to unfair treatment based on the physical characteristics of gender or race now clearly evident.[3]

Unlike gender- or race-based discrimination, however, age-based discrimination is often generated by those who one day will be its recipients. "It seems strange that young people would be prejudiced toward a group to which they will eventually belong," editor Todd D. Nelson astutely noted in the 2002 collection of essays *Ageism: Stereotyping and Prejudice Against Older Persons*, asking where this "negative affect" originates. Researchers had up to that point conducted a number of different studies to try to answer that good question, with various theories put forth based on the findings. Still, the definitive origins of ageism were elusive, the result of many different social factors in play. Nelson made "a loud and clear call to all prejudice researchers to examine the problem of ageism," thinking that "we have just begun to scratch the surface of this long-neglected area."[4]

Over the next couple of decades, not just "prejudice researchers" but people of many different backgrounds have devoted at least a portion of their careers and lives to address the problem of ageism in America. One of them is Margaret Morganroth Gullette, who calls herself not just a cultural critic but also an age critic. In her 2011 *Agewise: Fighting the New Ageism in America*, Gullette argued that Americans were (finally) becoming "agewise," i.e., sensitive to the discrimination faced by older people that was a part of everyday life. The 2009 movie *Up in the Air* in which a series of middle-aged employees get fired by the character played by George Clooney sparked real-life conversations about ageism in the workplace and what was euphemistically called "displacement." Shockingly, the Supreme Court had in 2000 ruled that "States may discriminate on the basis of age," leading Gullette to conclude that "practices that should be condemned are being institutionalized."[5]

Gullette continued to point out America's shameful and openly tolerated policies that have damaged the lives of millions of older people. In her wonderfully titled 2017 *Ending Ageism, or How Not to Shoot Old People*, Gullette again weighed in on what she called "the infliction of suffering by mere birthdate." Ageism was culturally defined, she emphasized, and the central theme of the narrative had declined significantly over the past century. There needed to be something equivalent to Martin Luther King Jr.'s "I Have a Dream" speech to make Americans rise up, Gullette felt, as only that had the potential to motivate enough citizens to engage in the struggle against ageism.[6]

Until somebody makes such a stirring speech, it's up to ordinary folks like us and some very smart people to do what we can to point out ageism when we see it and advocate for change. Fortunately, a growing number of researchers around the world are gravitating to the field as aging becomes a rather hot area within the social sciences. In their 2018 *Contemporary Perspectives on Ageism*, editors Liat Ayalon and Clemens Tesch-Romer gathered a group of scholars from 20 different countries and a wide variety of disciplines to offer their thoughts on the subject. Academics specializing in psychology, sociology, gerontology, geriatrics, pharmacology, law, geography, design, engineering, policy, and media studies contributed essays with the collective goal to suggest ways we can "reconstruct the image of old age." Although decidedly European-centric, the (open-access) textbook demonstrates the collaborative efforts being taken to address the origins, consequences, and potential responses to ageism.[7]

In her 2018 *Disrupt Aging: A Bold New Path to Living Your Best Life at Every Age*, Jo Ann Jenkins, the CEO of AARP, offers useful ways we can reconstruct the image of old age. Jenkins wisely suggests we stop fighting aging and instead fight ageism, as doing the latter will make it unnecessary to do the former. Many of us are not even aware that we're perpetuating ageist attitudes and behaviors, she points out, illustrating how deeply seated the problem really is. "We have to change the mindset and build an awareness of ageism to set the foundation for changing the social norms," Jenkins explains, with one good way being to make age discrimination equivalent to that based on race, gender, and sexual orientation. Beyond the issue of unfairness, ageism creates a negative view of aging, making it in the interests of all of us to speak out against it in order to eliminate it.[8]

Disrupting aging relies heavily on getting rid of the stereotypes that are firmly attached to getting older. In their 2020 *Getting Wise About Getting Old: Debunking Myths about Aging*, editors Veronique Billette, Patrik Marier, and Anne-Marie Seguin and their fellow essayists directly confront the various myths that support ageism's central narrative of decline. Older adults are not the idle, feeble, nonsexual, and intellectually rigid people they are often said to be (especially in the media), the contributors show through hard evidence, nor are they responsible for an upcoming economic apocalypse. Deconstructing such myths will indeed go a long way to ending ageism, a tall order that demands a powerful brand of activism.[9]

Enter Ashton Applewhite, probably the world's leading advocate for anti-ageism. Applewhite made a big splash with her 2020 *This Chair Rocks: A Manifesto Against Ageism* and even more so with her celebrated 2017 "Let's End Ageism" TED talk. (It was named one of the "50 Essential Civil Rights Speeches" by Stacker.com.) Applewhite took special aim at beauty and pharmaceutical companies, which, by marketing "anti-aging" products and services, are only further demonizing the natural process of aging. By presenting a positive view of aging, *This Chair Rocks* has been employed as a source of empowerment by its many readers and as an agent for social change. The book is "an important wake-up call for any baby boomer who's apprehensive about growing old," thought sociologist, sexologist, and AARP ambassador Pepper Schwartz, echoing Applewhite's call for "age pride!"[10]

The Cult of Youth

Demonstrating pride in one's age, whatever the number happens to be, is just the kind of rallying call needed to end ageism in America. The idea of an age-equal society in which all citizens—young, old, and in between—are respected and valued is no doubt a worthy pursuit that resonates with what the United States is supposed to be about. Indeed, around the world, Americans are widely considered a friendly people, a function perhaps of our democratic ideals, pluralistic population, and illusion that we're all somehow middle class. But is America "age friendly," i.e., inclusive toward older people as workers, consumers, and citizens?

Sadly, as the erudite students of ageism cited previously have made crystal clear, no. Although there are currently a greater number of older people in America than ever before in history, aging is seen in our society as a state of descent, the downward side of the curve of life. Despite attempts by AARP and some "pro-aging" advocates that should be applauded, the years following age 60 or even younger are commonly considered the period between the end of one's real, active life and death, making it a kind of existential purgatory. Older people are generally deemed weaker, less attractive versions of their younger selves, a terrible and simply untrue expression of identity.[11]

It is perhaps easy to see how older people are often viewed as little more than slow-walking, bad-driving, hard-of-hearing, *Matlock*-watching citizens. Studies show that negative attitudes toward older people are present in young children, and these feelings are difficult to change by the time they become tweens. Hollywood has been especially unfriendly toward older people, either portraying them as comic foils or ignoring them completely. This has reinforced cultural stereotypes related to aging and helped to make older people themselves lower their self-worth.[12]

Given this cultural orientation, it isn't surprising that baby boomers like myself are now increasingly the targets of ageism (thinking or believing in a negative manner about the process of becoming old or about old people). Ageism, which, it must be said, is both unethical and, when expressed in the workplace, illegal, can be seen as a predictable by-product of a culture in which getting older has little or no positive value. Our ageist society has deep roots, going back decades to produce what is perhaps the most youth-oriented culture in history. The idea and reality of aging have contradicted prevailing social values, attitudes, and beliefs, a phenomenon that has largely disenfranchised and marginalized older people from the rest of the population. One could reasonably conclude that the aging of what was the largest generation in history (until millennials came along) would have significantly altered American values over the last half-century, but this simply hasn't happened.[13]

Widespread ageism is a function of a variety of misperceptions grounded in our strange denial of the completely natural process of getting older. Aging as a whole is often viewed in the United States as something that happens to other people when, of course, it is, like birth and death, a universal experience. The aversion to, and even hatred of, older persons is all the more peculiar given that everyone will become one if he or she lives long enough. (The same cannot be true of racism or sexism, as people do not change color or, with relatively few exceptions, gender.)[14]

Other ways Americans distance themselves from aging is to think that individuals turn into different people when they get older or that the process takes place quite suddenly. A person is young and then boom—he or she is old—as this notion goes, a completely inaccurate reading of how humans actually—i.e., gradually—age. (As well, from a biological standpoint, each body part ages at a different rate depending on the individual, meaning there is no single physical process of aging.) Grouping people into an anonymous mass of "old people" is equally silly but not uncommon; 70-year-olds are just as individualistic as 30-year-olds (if not more so given the fact that they have had more time to develop their unique personalities). Finally, older people do not remain in a constant state of "oldness" but continually change, another fact that anyone younger than middle-aged might find hard to believe or accept.[15]

America was not always a youth-oriented culture, however. As I discussed in my cultural history of aging in America, people who lived a long life were venerated from the 17th through the early 19th centuries. Advanced age was seen as divinely ordained in part because it was comparatively rare; in 1790, for example, just 20% of the population lived to be 70 years old. That sentiment soon began to change, however; older people at the turn of the 19th century were not exalted as their parents and grandparents had been. Older Americans continued to lose social status as the "cult of youth" gained traction through the 19th century. By the 1920s, oldness in all forms was condemned in an increasingly modern society. Old people were considered a drag on the noble pursuit of progress, and more people were living longer, making old age less special than it had been a century earlier.[16]

Given this cultural climate, separating the old from the young seemed like a sensible idea. "Old age homes" became popular around the turn of the 20th century, a means to segregate people believed to be no longer capable of contributing to society. Forced retirement had already become common in many occupations in the latter 1800s, a reflection of Americans' negative attitudes toward older people. This "demotion" of older Americans soon became institutionalized and codified. By the end of World War I, aging was viewed as a social problem, and gerontology emerged as a professional field to help solve the perceived challenges of the elderly. As well, with older people generally no longer welcome in the workplace, the idea of providing pensions gained acceptance.[17]

Alongside this less than happy story was the good news that the average life span of Americans continued to increase. More years of retirement meant more money was required to pay old folks' living expenses, however—one of the downsides of greater longevity. The notion of saving for one's later years had not yet caught on, the basis for labor and politicians leading the way to provide support for older Americans via the Social Security Act of 1935. Attitudes toward older people thus began to become even more negative between the world wars. The Roaring Twenties had been a golden era for youth culture, of course, and the economic pressures of the Depression rewarded vitality and forward-thinking. Older people became increasingly defined as economically dependent on the government; while Social Security was a wonderful thing, it also helped to create the image of older Americans as unproductive and a costly drain on society.[18]

The narrative of ageism in America continued after World War II when aging became increasingly defined within the context of science and medicine. The postwar ethos that we could solve any problem if we put our minds to it served to further the perception that getting old was not unlike contracting a disease. Retirement was seen as a well-deserved rest and reward for older people after their vital and productive years, and the otherwise celebratory founding of AARP in 1958 could be said to have solidified retirement as a (final) stage of life. The spending of one's golden years, preferably in a warm place surrounded by other retirees, also operated as a convenient mechanism to put older people literally out of sight and mind. All of this contributed to the creation of a social construct of a group of citizens popularly labeled "seniors." Americans aged 65 years old or more increasingly became seen as a kind of special interest group separate from the rest of the population. Life was meaningless for those no longer working, many believed, justification for the trivializing and belittling of older people in common discourse. While grandma and grandpa certainly seemed happy in Florida or Arizona, a life of leisure was seen as a wasted one in postwar America since it ran contrary to the principles of free enterprise and upward mobility.[19]

While a noble pursuit, President Johnson's "Great Society" programs also contributed to cutting off older citizens from younger ones. The Older Americans Act of 1965 offered comprehensive services for older citizens, and Medicare and Medicaid programs began that same year, casting seniors as a costly expense of taxpayers' money. At the same time, the field of geriatric medicine expanded, formalizing what could legitimately be called an aging "industry." The rise of gerontology and social policies was thus a devil's bargain; older people benefited financially and in terms of longevity, but at the same time these developments helped to instill a negative view of older Americans. Focusing on the physical and cognitive problems of aging transformed older Americans into a group seen as requiring special care. The vastly improved medical and economic conditions for older people were accompanied by cultural disenfranchisement, the backdrop for today's virulent ageism in many spheres of everyday life.[20] Butler's coining of the term "ageism" came just three years after the passage of the Older Americans Act of 1965 and one year after Congress passed the Age Discrimination in Employment Act (ADEA), a telling sign that governmental legislation was not going to solve the problem.

Organized activism to combat ageism arguably began a couple of years later in Philadelphia with the formation of the Gray Panthers. The mission of the organization (whose name was inspired by the militant Black Panthers) was to dispel stereotypes about older people and to influence legislation affecting them. There were about 8,000 Gray Panthers in the United States by the nation's bicentennial, each member committed to fighting prejudice against older people and to bringing attention to their cause. Activism centered around the "three H's"—health, hunger, and housing—with much of it directed at the Ford administration's budget cutting as it dismantled a good part of LBJ's "Great Society" programs.[21]

Aging Is a Privilege

The entry of "anti-aging" onto the health and beauty scene has only contributed to America's ugly history of ageism. You can become "ageless," declares quite a number of cosmetics marketers making the promise that their product has some kind of de-aging properties. Scientists, or more likely actors playing scientists, tout the claims of these products that promise to make their users look and feel years or decades younger. Anti-aging is really two things: (1) the use of products that promise to make one appear younger and (2) the belief that one can live further, perhaps much further beyond the current life expectancy (about 76 for men and 81 for women in the United States). Even my beloved PBS station tells me I can "age backward," suggesting I can not only stop the effect of time on my body but also put it in reverse gear.

According to statista.com, the global beauty- and wellness-oriented anti-aging market was estimated to be worth about $58.5 billion dollars in 2020 and was forecast to grow 7% over the next five years.[22] Skin remedies—nightly "wrinkle repair" and "micro-sculpting" creams and moisturizers—are a big part of this market, but many other products and services, including dietary supplements, make up the huge business. It's clear that many people around the world want to make themselves look and feel younger or dramatically extend their life span. I'm naturally skeptical of any and all such claims, as I am of the belief that my body will continue to insist on aging regardless of the application or consumption of an alleged miraculous ingredient. Others, however, are willing to pay big bucks or restrict their lifestyles in the hope that the claims have some validity. (A 500 ml jar of Crème de la Mer, which "visibly reduces the size of pores" by means of an ingredient called Miracle Broth™, retails for $2,160, quite a price to pay for a younger-looking face.) Gobbling down large quantities of vitamins and supplements, passing on the carbs and meat, regularly exercising, and avoiding exposure to radiation exposure are all common steps taken to extend longevity.[23]

Although anti-aging products emerged in the 1980s, when baby boomers began hitting "the big 4–0," the desire to preserve one's youthfulness is hardly new. It is likely a myth that the Spanish conquistador sailed to what would become Florida to discover a fountain of youth, but the idea of delaying or reversing aging goes back thousands of years. All kinds of treatments have throughout history been used (some quite exotic), but none has been proven to work (save for the possible exception of severe calorie restriction). Given the physical and cognitive changes that typically occur as one gets older, it's perhaps understandable why so many of us are attracted to such treatments. ("Aging isn't for sissies," I sometimes hear.) That death always follows aging is yet more incentive to do whatever it takes to stop the body from what it is programmed to do. Much has been made of the idea that aging is a disease that can be cured, an argument David Sinclair makes in his *Lifespan: Why We Age and Why We Don't Have To*. Channeling Ray Kurzweil's *Fantastic Voyage: Live Long Enough to Live Forever*, Sinclair uses his own body to test his theories, but again there's no scientific basis for radical life extension regardless of how much ginkgo that we consume or how many shiatsu massages we get.[24]

While rubbing in a pricy lotion on one's face or choosing a different menu item than fettucine Bolognese is seemingly harmless, the social effects of anti-aging run much deeper. Beyond the fact that anti-aging beautification is scientifically baseless, the promotion of the concept is inherently ageist, as it casts getting older as a negative experience and older people as unattractive and unhealthy. Likewise, those arguing that aging is a disease are by default demonizing the process of becoming older, turning the entirely natural development of wrinkles, gray hair, and all the other biological markers of age into enemies to try to conquer (even if it takes out some of the joy of living). Rather than embrace aging as a normal and positive thing (the alternative being death), in other words, we are being told to fight aging off as long as we can and, if possible, make the inconvenient truth go away.

This is not just a bad message to hear but an anti-human one that is doing much to encourage ageist thinking and practices. "If the beauty industry is any indication, the whole world seems to believe that aging is a bad thing," noted curology.com, correctly thinking instead that "aging is a privilege." Women are the primary target of skin creams and, through language and imagery, marketers tap into their fears of being deemed less attractive and less desirable people in our society in which youth still prevails in terms of bodily aesthetics. Even though just the opposite is true—older women are more mature, confident, and powerful than when they were younger—the anti-aging narrative is about decline and irrelevance, contributing to and reinforcing ageist beliefs and actions.[25]

Fortunately, a backlash against anti-aging is in the works, one being led by a surprising source. In September 2017, *Allure* magazine, a publication known for telling readers how to be, well, more alluring, broke with the ranks by committing to no longer use the term "anti-aging." Editor Michelle Lee wrote that it was time for a "celebration of growing into your own skin—wrinkles and all," seemingly either a brave decision that might alienate advertisers or a clever marketing ploy to get media attention and perhaps take advantage of an aging reader base. *Allure* emphasized its message by putting 72-year-old Helen Mirren on the cover, labeling her as "the hero we need." Lee made it clear that the magazine would not stop promoting products that claim they can make women appear younger but rather change the way that it discussed aging. Indeed, in the very same issue, readers could see an ad for a new L'Oréal moisturizer that "stimulates cell turnover from within" so that users could "get [their] rosy tone back." And who was featured in the ad? Helen Mirren.[26]

While *Allure* was obviously sending a literally mixed message by simultaneously challenging and endorsing anti-aging, introducing the conversation into the beauty community and larger society was a step in the right direction. (The magazine's action was widely covered by the general media.) The mainstreaming of Botox had by then made anti-aging uncool and, more importantly, served as visible evidence of how fighting the physical effects of aging was ultimately a losing battle. It remains to be determined whether we've turned a corner in our attitudes about getting older (anti-aging beauty products are as popular as ever, as is the effort to extend our lives through radical therapies), but at least there are signs that an "anti-anti-aging" movement may be in the wings.[27]

The irony is that, because it is a tacit endorsement of ageism, anti-aging can negatively affect older people's health and actually shorten one's life. In a Yale

University longitudinal and cross-cultural study published in 2020, researchers found that there was a direct connection between age discrimination and other forms of ageism and the incidence of physical and mental illnesses. Decreased longevity was another outcome of ageist practices, a result of being denied health care, exclusion from clinical trials, and limited employment opportunities. Embracing aging and affording older people equal rights is not just the right thing to do from an ethical and moral perspective but also good medicine.[28]

The Demographic Cliff

The myths that surround the human aging process are not just the building blocks of ageism but the basis for us to fear the eventuality of getting older. Popular culture reinforces these fears, often in what is intended to be comedic fodder. Stroll down the birthday card aisle of a store and you're likely to see a considerable number of them poking good fun of the advanced age of the intended receiver, for example, especially at the onset of a new decade of aging such as 50, 60, or 70. Hope you're ready for frailty and infirmity, some cards might inform the now depressed birthday boy or girl, the all-in-good-fun jest part of the cultural trope that a half-century-or-more-old body had plenty of wear and tear. The truth, however, is that not much muscle function and cardiovascular fitness will disappear if one does some consistent strength or aerobic training, according to wellness experts, a less funny but more scientific observation. Also, they point out, it's never really too late to begin getting in shape, another blow to the inevitability of physical decline.[29]

The myth of universal cognitive decline—specifically the loss of memory—among older adults is another staple of everyday discourse. Having a "senior moment"—and "Why exactly did I come into this room?" we may ask—is cause for considerable concern among those of us who've been informed in so many words that we'll all ultimately have Alzheimer's or some other form of dementia. Blood flow to the brain does indeed tend to diminish with age, affecting some cognitive functioning, but semantic memory—how to do things and remember facts—typically stays robust. (A 65-year-old typically scores better on a vocabulary test than a 20-year-old.) Commercials hawking magical pills and all kinds of other products to allegedly help "brain health" reinforce the myth that older people are destined to become forgetful and senile, thereby contributing to ageist thinking and practices.[30]

Older adults are also commonly mislabeled as uncurious and uncreative people who are generally incapable of innovative thought, this despite the high number of artists and writers who produced great things in their 60s, 70s, and 80s. In fact, neuroscientists point out, changes to the brains of older people may make it more conducive to come up with new and original ideas. (It has something to do with frontal lobes.) Many retirees who spent their careers as lawyers, bankers, and accountants are finding new life painting, sculpting, salsa dancing, or doing some other right-brain pursuit, their latent creative talent having lain dormant for decades.[31]

The myth that older people are as a rule nonsexual has also contributed to pervasive ageist attitudes. We connect sexuality with beauty, the standards of which have been grounded in smooth skin and other signs of youthfulness. We may not like to think of a couple of septuagenarians, well, coupling, but the truth is there's a lot of action going on in retirement communities. The frequency of sexual activity when one is older is a function of how sexual one was as a younger person, aging experts explain. And as with any endeavor, aging brings experience to sexuality, perhaps giving those who've been around the block a few times an edge in that department.[32]

Another running joke is the all-thumbs, analogical geezer trying to use his or her mobile phone, tablet, or some other tech-intense device. The reality is that older adults are frequent users of technology when it helps them do what they want to get done. "Despite the attention the digital divide has garnered, a large proportion of older adults use technology to maintain their social networks and make their lives easier," said William Chopik, an assistant professor of psychology at Michigan State University, after coauthoring a study on the subject. Prevailing thought dictates that older people only use their computers to check in with their grandchildren on Facebook, but Chopik's study found that the former frequently used various social media platforms for the same reasons the latter did.[33]

While such myths are obviously problematic, there is an underlying "metamyth" that is fueling ageism by the casting of older people as a villainous threat to the global economy. The world's aging population spells economic doom to us all, this story goes, the sheer numbers of humans that are currently climbing and will soon fall over the "demographic cliff" to wreak life as we know it. No doubt, the world is aging, and fast, as the 65-and-older segment of the population rises not just in the United States but Europe and Asia as well. The postwar baby boom combined with lower birth rates and greater longevity is a perfect recipe for such a shift, making many believe there is an apocalyptic scenario on the horizon. Who's going to do all the work? Who's going to pay all those old folks' medical bills? Naturally, baby boomers are responsible for the demographic time bomb that is ticking, making them the blame for the crisis that is quickly approaching.[34]

The problem with the story, like other ageist myths, is that it simply isn't true. Aging societies are not worse off economically, the facts show, with little reason to believe they will ever be so. In fact, the prospect of a very large force of older workers is a good thing, if employers could get over their Eisenhower-era thinking that anyone over 65 years old should be sent packing to Retirement Village. "New technologies and business policies might keep talented people working longer," David Rotman wrote in the *MIT Technology Review* in 2019, thinking that "teams made of both young and old people, with diverse experience, might even be more productive." Perceiving the aging population as a potentially positive scenario versus an inevitably negative one is the key to dispelling this uber-myth, an admittedly difficult thing to do given the brand of ageism now being directed at baby boomers.[35]

A Vast and Strange Generation

Ageism is in part a function of a younger generation holding negative feelings toward an older generation. It should not be news that many members of Generation X and Generation Y (millennials) dislike if not despise baby boomers and everything the latter stand for. While their relative merit is up for debate, it can't be argued that boomers (who are currently in their late 50s to mid-70s) are a unique generation. This is a direct result of their shared experiences of having been born in postwar America and being part of or exposed to the counterculture in their youth. Generational (and generalized) traits include an orientation toward prosperity and abundance, a consumerist ethos, a comfort with peer pressure, an acceptance of great expectations, an acquaintance with social and political turmoil (the civil rights and feminist movements, Vietnam, assassinations, Watergate), an idealist philosophy, a rebellious streak and a distrust of institutions, a generally liberal social attitude, and a leaning toward all things creative. Because of these traits and having spent their formative years in what was unarguably a special time and place from a historical perspective, boomers believe they were and remain a chosen people of sorts.

Many Gen Xers and Gen Yers, however, perceive baby boomers in much less flattering terms. Boomers hogged the economy and the world's resources for their own financial gain and/or consumptive habits, I've been repeatedly told; my cohort is often seen as greedy and wasteful, with no regard for what future generations will inherit. To put it another way, boomers are frequently viewed as dinner guests who've eaten and drank pretty much everything set out on the table, leaving only scraps for those who came later to the party (even their own children). In short, the sorry state of the world, including global warming, is considered to be largely their fault.

The backdrop to this kind of thinking is that baby boomers unquestionably dominated American society during the 1980s and 1990s (the "yuppie" and "post-yuppie" eras) as they advanced professionally. The sheer numbers and collective wealth of the generation dwarfed that of Gen X, making boomers a convenient target among those feeling that the economic cards were unevenly dealt. Boomers' undeniably aspirational, often competitive, instincts have helped to inform such a view, as has their unapologetic inclination to buy things they don't really need and soon get rid of so they can buy something new—an unsustainable proposition.

Generational hostility is nothing new. There is, in fact, a long history in America of a younger generation differentiating and distancing itself from its parents' generation. (It actually goes back to the 18th century.) As a people, we are very much interested in making our own mark, blazing our own trail, and doing things our own way. From this respect, it was inevitable that Gen Xers would set themselves off from baby boomers and attempt to carve out their collective identity. The same was and remains true for millennials and Gen Z.

That said, there seems to be a special effort being made by many Gen Xers and millennials to create a contentious relationship with boomers. I consider this to be a kind of "hyper-ageism" in which older people are not just viewed in negative terms but also in antagonistic ones.

Do baby boomers deserve the criticism they regularly receive? Full disclosure: I am unapologetically pro-boomer, a not surprising thing given that I was born in the sweet spot of the birth spike of the generation that came to be known as baby boomers because of their high numbers. As well, I have some personal experience with pretty much all of the seminal moments (most notably duck-and-cover drills, the Beatles' first appearance on *The Ed Sullivan Show*, the assassinations of JFK, MLK, and RFK, the first moon landing, and the counterculture era's final hurrah, Woodstock) that are commonly associated with the group. This historical legacy has become so familiar that it understandably seems like to some a documentary that they have watched too many times, part of the reason for the widespread antipathy directed at the group. Boomer bashing has long been in vogue, of course, with the "Me Generation" earning its selfish reputation in the hedonistic 1970s and its greed-is-good image in the materialistic 1980s.

Recently, however, criticism directed toward baby boomers has become especially nasty, a by-product of the negative feelings many younger people have about older people in general. Some historically challenged Gen Xers and millennials do not just dismiss older Americans' unsurpassed contributions to society that continue to this day but fully believe boomers were the worst generation in history. (Just Google "baby boomers" if you have any doubt about this.) Bruce Gibney is the undisputed champion of boomer bashing, as his 2017 book *A Generation of Sociopaths: How the Baby Boomers Betrayed America* makes clear. "For the past several decades, the nation has been run by people who present, personally and politically, the full sociopathic pathology: deceit, selfishness, imprudence, remorseless, hostility," Gibney writes in the very first paragraph, labeling boomers a "vast and strange generation."[36] (The magazine *Lawyers, Guns and Money* considered the book "intellectually invaluable," this despite the fact that Gibney begins the baby boom era as 1940 rather than the correct 1946.)

If baby boomers' collective past has been portrayed as economically and environmentally disastrous, according to such critics, their future is nothing short of apocalyptic. Because of their numbers and greedy tendencies, this theory goes (backed up by many economists), boomers will wreck the American economy and health-care system as they age, with millennials having to pick up the tab. Some go even further by saying it's due time that boomers just got out of the way and allow younger generations to make their own mark in society, a classic case of ageism that has no place in American society. Putting older people on an ice flow to let them float away, as the (factually false) Eskimo legend goes, would seem to suit such boomer bashers just fine.

Often overlooked in such erroneous accusations and misinformed predictions are the startling array of achievements baby boomers have realized since the first one was born three-quarters of a century ago. Growing up in the Cold War, when it was commonly believed that the world could blow up at any point, gave boomers a sense of urgency to accomplish great things, many of which they actually did. Boomers fought bravely in the Vietnam War, led a cultural revolution grounded in the noble ideas of peace and equality, and then embarked on careers that propelled this nation to become the most powerful and wealthiest in civilization. Along the way, they popularized if not downright invented things like rock 'n roll, the computer, and the Internet, all the while giving more money away to worthy causes than any previous generation. There is no doubt that boomers were undeniably fortunate to have come of age during the latter half of the amazing "American Century"; they greatly benefited from the incredible scientific and technological strides made in the postwar years and happened to be in the right place at the right time when the nation was ready to reinvent itself in the late sixties. Launching and continuing their careers in the economically advantageous 1980s and 1990s was also perfect timing, and the steadily upward tick of the stock market and escalation of real estate prices over the last decade and a half has only added to the net worth of many boomers.

While this is admittedly a rejoinder against the rising tide of vitriol directed at the group, I fully recognize that the generation has not fully lived up to its potential. Many have abused their physical selves in a manner to make them as a group less healthy than they could and perhaps should have been at an advanced age given their obsession with "naturalness" when young. ("I would have treated my body better had I known I would have lived this long" is a commonly heard refrain.) As well, boomers certainly took conspicuous consumption to an entirely new level, fueling our dominant earn-and-spend ethos. Until recently, boomers failed to form any kind of significant coalition to fight virulent ageism, instead futilely trying to hang on to the remnants of their rapidly fading youth. Now, however, many are combating ageism much like how they confronted racial and gender prejudice and an unjust war in their first and second acts, reinvigorating their roots in social activism.

OK Boomer

Ageism is of course not just an American problem but a global one. Countries around the world have acknowledged how their respective nation should become more age friendly now and in the future. "With the global population of older adults set to double to 2 billion by 2050, world leaders increasingly recognize that this demographic shift requires fundamental changes from businesses, governments and economies," Michael W. Hodin, CEO at the Global Coalition on Aging and managing partner at High Lantern Group, noted in *Aging Today* in 2019. Hodin had just returned from the Silver Economy Forum in Helsinki, where five big ideas emerged, the first being "Out with Ageism." The WHO has called ageism "the most socially acceptable prejudice in the world," which affects people old and young. WHO has led international efforts to combat ageism, going as far as to declare the years 2020 to 2030 to be the "Decade of Healthy Ageing."[37]

With research already showing that the various expressions of ageism can negatively impact both mental and physical health, WHO is taking an active role in addressing its many challenges. In 2019, the organization kicked off no less than four studies designed to define ageism and identify ways to fight it. In 2017, WHO had published a report titled "Global Strategy and Action Plan on Aging and Health," but there was much more work to be done. "It's an incredibly prevalent and insidious problem," said Alana Officer, who headed up the organization's global campaign against ageism, which it defines as "stereotyping, prejudice and discrimination" based on age. "It affects not only individuals, but how we think about policies," she added, justification for four teams (including one from Cornell University) to determine both the causes and consequences of ageism. The findings would be published in a United Nations report and then, hopefully, serve as a foundation for change.[38]

It should be said that geriatricians have developed various successful models of hospital care for older adults. The larger goal, however, is to create a better framework to manage the health care of a rapidly aging population, an ambitious but much-needed pursuit. In 2016, the John A. Hartford Foundation partnered with the Institute for Healthcare Improvement to forge the "Age-Friendly Health Systems" initiative that focused on the "4Ms" of age-friendly care: what matters most to patients (sharing goals and priorities), medication (a review of everything being taken), mentation (talking about memory and mood), and mobility (asking about ways to help keep one active and moving).[39] The 4Ms define care that meets the needs of a patient not just in the hospital but also to enhance their daily lives, something that should lessen ageist thinking and practices in health care. More health systems, hospitals, and medical practices across the country are adopting the initiative and its 4Ms.[40]

Despite the great value of the 4Ms, there is considerable evidence that ageism is institutionally embedded in health-care systems themselves. A range of discriminatory practices including overtreatment, undertreatment, and lower rates of screening tests and other preventive interventions like vaccination are not uncommon, according to Paula R. DeCola, senior director and Global Patient Affairs and Global Lead at the Pfizer Center of Excellence on Active and Healthy Ageing. Clinical research too is biased, those in the health-care field have found, with older people often excluded from trials because of their age. Older adults would participate in clinical trials if informed of them, it was learned, but that doesn't happen often. "Patients, healthcare professionals and the pharmaceutical industry must foster the activation of older people," DeCola wrote in *Aging Today* in 2018, concluding that, "ageism is bad for our health."[41]

That even the health-care industry can adversely affect older people's well-being through ageism shows how deeply it runs through society. The truth is that most of those in their third act have a positive view about getting older, but you certainly wouldn't know that by the constant stream of ageist conversation and media imagery that are part of daily life. People in their 70s can't use a smartphone, we might hear, or be told one of the many jokes about the geezer who is forgetful or deaf. "Everyday ageism is part of American culture and one of the most common and socially condoned forms of prejudice and discrimination," stated Julie Ober Allen, a research fellow at the University of Michigan Institute for Social Research, in 2020. Allen was part of a team who conducted a survey called the National Poll on Healthy Aging; the findings showed there was a correlation between ageism and health problems. Although 88% of those polled said they had become more comfortable "being themselves," more than a third reported having internalized stereotypes about oldness that had led to some loneliness or depression.[42]

Quite depressing is the "ok boomer" mini-movement that has further embedded ageist stereotypes and fueled the generational divide. Blaming baby boomers for climate change, financial inequality, and political corruption, some members of Gen Z (those born roughly between 1995 and 2010) have adopted the phrase "ok boomer," meaning people of that older generation just don't get it. Anyone who appears to be of a certain age and says something condescending about young people or the things that are important to them (especially in a

YouTube and TikTok video) is subject to being "ok boomered." Teenagers have been known to write the phrase down in various places (including on themselves), and merchandise bearing the words are available for sale. "It's the digital equivalent of an eye roll," as Lorenz Taylor described it in the *New York Times* in 2019, in that sense perhaps not much different than the sentiment many baby boomers felt toward the Silent Generation in the 1960s.[43]

Happily, some innovative steps toward bridging generational differences and combating everyday ageism have been taken. One of the most interesting was the Masonicare-Quinnipiac University Students in Residence Program which literally brought together younger and older people to find common ground. The program had students from the university actually live at Masonicare at Ashlar Village, a retirement community in Wallingford, Connecticut, for the 2017–2018 academic year. While intergenerational learning is not uncommon—there are dozens of assisted living facilities on university campuses and many colleges that allow older adults to take classes at no or low cost—just a few have the generations live together. The goal of the Masonicare-Quinnipiac program is to defuse generational stereotypes, something that can go a long way to lessening ageism throughout society. Some of the students in the program are considering careers based in gerontology or geriatrics, such as elder law, giving them firsthand knowledge of the kind of work they may be doing.[44]

The program sparked some fascinating interchanges. One 21-year-old female student became a close friend of a 91-year-old woman in the community; the two spent hours talking to each other about everything from boyfriends to baking and stayed friends. "She's not like another grandma," the student later told a newspaper reporter. "She's just one of the girls."

"It's nice to have someone come in who's young, who is vibrant, who smiles, who talks to us," said an 85-year-old resident, finding considerable value in having people more than 60 years her junior around all the time.

The students learn much from the older residents (some of whom had careers as scientists and medical professionals), seeing them as living history lessons. Another program had students from the Cleveland Institute of Music live at the Judson Manor retirement home in that city with similar positive results. Considering its program to be a success, a Quinnipiac University official was thinking about placing one of the Masonicare residents in a dorm, that too likely to debunk some of the myths surrounding both younger and older people.[45]

Interestingly, some universities are building facilities for people to live in as retirement communities, an attractive option for many baby boomers seeking an alternative to aging in place in their existing homes or moving to the traditional gated-development-in-a-warm-place setting. Intergenerational and offering the opportunity for lifelong learning, college campuses do indeed appear to be an ideal place to settle for a generation that has always prized education and will be perpetually youthful in spirit, if not body.

Younger Minds

If only such intergenerational amity could be found in the American workplace. Given the average advanced age of a newly appointed judge serving on the U.S. Supreme Court (currently 52) and that judges normally serve for about 20 years, one might reasonably conclude that laws concerning discrimination at work would support the rights of older employees. This simply isn't the case and has never been so. It's disturbing to think of the highest court in the land as an ageist organization, but the facts speak for themselves. The Court's 2000 decision to allow states to discriminate on the basis of age was bad enough, but in 2009, the wise elders doubled down by making it more difficult for employees and job applicants to prove age discrimination. In *Gross v. FBL Financial Services*, the Court stated that a plaintiff had to show that age was the deciding (versus motivating) factor for an employer taking adverse action against a current or prospective worker. The Court's decision effectively allowed a certain amount of age discrimination to legally exist, a wrong and ridiculous thing when considered within the context of our principles rooted in fairness and equality at work and everywhere else. Congressional acts in the 1960s also did no favors to older Americans in terms of discrimination at work, making one wonder if the federal government as a whole endorses ageism.[46]

Regardless, all kinds of ageist practices and policies are embedded in American work culture, especially when hiring new talent. The seeking of "digital natives," for example, is inherently ageist, as only younger generations have grown up with online technology. Similarly, while recruiting on college campuses and searching for "recent college graduates" is legal, it intentionally creates an ageist imbalance in most companies. Capping years of experience, say five to ten, is another clever means of preventing older adults from getting hired. Do any organizations purposely recruit for older adults, advertise for "non-recent college graduates," or take a the-more-experience-the-better approach? Of course not, making it not surprising that the ranks of corporations are filled with 20- and 30-somethings, making the relatively few 50-something and 60-somethings feel like unwelcome guests. Let's just say it for what it is: millennials are enjoying the big party being held in Corporate America, and they don't want their parents or people who look like them to crash it and ruin the good times.[47]

Given essentially free rein over the constitutional rights of older workers, Big Business has taken deliberate steps to keep them out of the American workforce. In 2018, the Communication Workers of America union expanded the class action suit they had previously filed against some of the nation's top employers. Companies including Amazon, T-Mobile, Capital One, Enterprise Rent-A-Car were accused of intentionally profiling their advertising on Facebook to exclude older people, a classic case of ageism. IBM had been deaccessioning thousands of older employees for years, an investigation revealed, and, based on the number of lawsuits being filed in Silicon Valley, the tech industry had earned a deserved reputation for age discrimination. (Seven out of 18 top Silicon Valley companies have a median age of 30 or younger.) It's obvious that the Age Discrimination Employment Act of 1967 is as dated as an IBM Selectric typewriter and that the nation's laws regarding the legal rights of older workers need to be brought into the 21st century.[48]

Given our ageist cultural climate and lack of legal support, an older adult's applying and (if lucky) interviewing for a job is a harrowing process. Email a resume to a company, and there's a distinct chance it will never reach an actual human being, having been instantly rejected by software designed to spot a person a half-century old or older. College degrees awarded often carry dates, and decades of experience, too, are clues to an applicant's age. While older workers are commonly seen as less effective and less efficient, they're also viewed by some younger workers as a competitive threat who may rise faster through the ranks (and possibly be their boss one day). Because top management, having more experience, is often older, a concerted effort is made to prevent middle-aged people from entering organizations as new hires. Needless to say, this is unfair and discriminatory, as a 50-year-old needs to pay his or her bills just as much as a 30-year-old. Moreover, older workers have a strong work ethic, are loyal to their employers, and are more likely to be satisfied with their jobs than their younger coworkers, according to research from the Stanford Center on Longevity, yet more reasons why age discrimination in the workplace makes no sense.[49]

Although most managers know better, some are not shy about telling job candidates that, in so many words, they're too old to be hired. An experienced worker might in an interview hear that the company is looking for "younger minds," while another may think it odd that the Human Resources person is curious to know if that candidate's kids are in college. (One person informed me that in an interview, she was told flat out that she was a "dinosaur.") Executive coaches and the like offer all kinds of tips to try to skirt ageism when interviewing for a job (i.e., focusing on "energy" versus experience and dressing for success), but that is missing the larger point: age should not be considered and used as a determining factor in qualifying for any job.[50]

Following the U.S. Supreme Court's lead, lower courts are expressing tolerance toward ageism in the workplace. In the Eighth U.S. Circuit Court of Appeals in 2019, for example, a three-judge panel ruled that the federal ADEA does not apply to partnerships. The case involved a 72-year-old lawyer who was terminated based on the firm's mandatory age 70 retirement policy. The man had worked at the St. Louis law firm for 45 years, but the court decided that because he was a partner, he did not qualify as an employee, whom the 1967 act was intended to protect. The decision was important in that it constituted a binding precedent for a seven-state region and could very well influence circuit courts across the nation. As well, the decision affected not just law firms but also any kind of professional services partnerships, including medical clinics, accounting and financial advisories, and architectural firms. With the ruling, it was now entirely legal for a partner in those states to be told, "We're firing you because you're too old."[51]

Can't we do better than this? Is the intent of our legal system to allow any form of discrimination in the workplace or anywhere else? Can one imagine the repercussions if an employee was told, "We're firing you because you're black/female/gay/disabled"? Ageism is such a pervasive force in American culture that even our courts endorse it, offering considerable truth that discrimination against older people is the last form of inequality that is allowed to openly exist. As Americans, it's our responsibility to see ageism as just as bad as racism and do whatever we can to stop it in its tracks. Ageism, like all other dictatorial isms, has no place in this country.

Fortunately, measures are being taken to equate age discrimination in the workplace to other forms of bias. AARP, not surprisingly, is serving as the loudest voice of ageism and using its immense resources to try to, as the organization often says, "disrupt the narrative" of aging. In 2020, AARP published the results of a study conducted by the Economist Intelligence Unit; its findings showed that age discrimination against workers went well beyond a 72-year-old lawyer getting fired because, while helping his law firm make money for the past 45 years, he got old. Workplace ageism had a negative impact on the nation's entire economy, the study reported, costing the country billions of dollars that would have been generated had more age 50-plus workers been given the jobs they wanted and deserved. Unemployment, underemployment, and involuntary retirement of older workers were pervasive practices despite the fact that there is much evidence showing that these very same people bring valuable skills, knowledge, and perspective to businesses and the economy.[52]

AARP is not just talking the talk but taking action against such un-American activity. "We need to challenge workplace policies that force older workers to retire before they are ready," Jo Ann Jenkins wrote in 2020, "we must change outdated stereotypes that keep older workers from taking new jobs or continuing to rise in the ones they have." To that point, Jenkins and her colleagues are lobbying for passage of the Protecting Older Workers Against Discrimination Act (POWADA), a bipartisan bill that would give older workers the same legal protections against age discrimination as those that exist for discrimination based on race, gender, nationality, and religion. The act was passed by the U.S. House of Representatives, and AARP was urging the Senate to push it through. If enacted, POWADA would grant the rights that were restricted by the 2009 Supreme Court decision making it difficult if not impossible to legally demonstrate age-based workplace discrimination. "As people live longer, they are eager to continue working," Jenkins noted, adding, "when that happens, we all win."[53]

Notes

1 Daniel Bates, "Jagger and Strolling Bones Accused of Ageism," *Daily Mail*, December 29, 2018.

2 Robert N. Butler, MD., *Why Survive? Being Old in America* (New York: Harper & Row, 1975) xi–xii.

3 Howard Chudacoff, *How Old Are You? Age Consciousness in America* (Princeton, NJ: Princeton University Press, 1989) 4–6, 186–187.

4 Todd D. Nelson, ed., *Ageism: Stereotyping and Prejudice Against Older Persons* (Cambridge, MA: MIT Press, 2002) x, xiii.

5 Margaret Morganroth Gullette, *Agewise: Fighting the New Ageism in America* (Chicago: University of Chicago Press, 2011) 1–4.

6 Margaret Morganroth Gullette, *Ending Ageism, or How Not to Shoot Old People* (New Brunswick, NJ: Rutgers University Press, 2017) xii–xiii.

7 Liat Ayalon and Clemens Tesch-Romer, eds., *Contemporary Perspectives on Ageism* (New York: Springer, 2018).

8 Jo Ann Jenkins, *Disrupt Aging: A Bold New Path to Living Your Best Life at Every Age* (New York: Public Affairs, 2018) 39–40.

9 Veronique Billette, Patrik Marier, and Anne-Marie Seguin, eds., *Getting Wise About Getting Old: Debunking Myths about Aging* (Vancouver, BC: University of British Columbia Press, 2020).

10 Ashton Applewhite, *This Chair Rocks: A Manifesto Against Ageism* (New York: Celadon Books, 2020).

11 Lawrence R. Samuel, *Aging in America: A Cultural History* (Philadelphia: University of Pennsylvania Press, 2017).

12 *Aging in America.*

13 *Aging in America.*

14 *Aging in America.*

15 *Aging in America.*

16 *Aging in America.*

17 *Aging in America.*

18 *Aging in America.*

19 *Aging in America.*

20 *Aging in America.*

21 *Aging in America.*

22 statista.com.

23 Harriet Hall, MD., "The Fountain of Youth and Other Anti-Aging Myths," *Skeptic Magazine*, 2000, 4.

24 "The Fountain of Youth and Other Anti-Aging Myths."

25 Curology Team, "Ageism and Anti-aging: Think Differently about Wrinkle Prevention," *blog.curology.com*, April 11, 2019.

26 Amanda Hess, "Old Money," *New York Times*, September 17, 2017, SM13.

27 "Old Money."

28 Alice Park, "How Ageism Negatively Affects Older People's Health," *Time.com*, January 21, 2020.

29 Jen McCaffery, "5 Myths About Aging," *Prevention*, April 2017, 34–37.

30 "5 Myths About Aging."

31 "5 Myths About Aging."

32 "5 Myths About Aging."

33 "5 Myths About Aging."

34 David Rotman, "Don't Fear the Gray Tsunami," *MIT Technology Review*, August 21, 2019, 8–9.

35 "Don't Fear the Gray Tsunami."

36 Bruce Gibney, *A Generation of Sociopaths: How the Baby Boomers Betrayed America* (New York: Hachette, 2017).

37 Michael W. Hodin, "The Future's So Bright: The Top 5 Takeaways from the Silver Economy Forum," *Aging Today*, September/October 2019, 11.

38 Paula Span, "Ageism: A 'Prevalent and Insidious' Health Threat: The New Old Age," *New York Times (Online)*, April 26, 2019.

39 webmd.com.

40 Michele Cohen Marill, "Age-Friendly Care at the Emergency Department," *Health Affairs*, November 2019, 1780–1785.

41 Paula R. DeCola, "Ageism Hinders Clinical Trials—and Our Health," *Aging Today*, September/October 2018, 16.

42 "Seniors Report Experiencing 'Everyday' Ageism," *Journal of Business (Spokane, WA)*, July 30, 2020, 27.

43 Lorenz Taylor, "Ok Boomer Marks the End of Friendly Generational Relations," *New York Times*, November 4, 2019.

44 Pat Robb-Eaton, "Program Combats Ageism by Having Students Live with Seniors," *Telegraph-Herald (Dubuque, Iowa)*, August 25, 2018, X2.

45 "Program Combats Ageism by Having Students Live with Seniors."

46 Katie Loehrke, "Are Your Hiring Practices Overtly (or Covertly) Discriminatory?" *Buffalo Law Journal*, March 19, 2018, 9.

47 "Are Your Hiring Practices Overtly (or Covertly) Discriminatory?"

48 Chip Conley, "How Do We Combat Ageism? By Valuing Wisdom as Much as Youth," *Harvard Business Review,* June 21, 2018.

49 Rebecca Zucker, "5 Ways to Respond to Ageism in a Job Interview," *Harvard Business Review,* August 2, 2019.

50 "5 Ways to Respond to Ageism in a Job Interview."

51 Marshall H. Tanick, "Perspectives: Boomers, Beware That Age Bias Law Might Not Work," *Minnesota Lawyer,* January 7, 2020.

52 Jo Ann Jenkins, "Age Bias Costs Us All," *AARP Bulletin,* March 2020.

53 "Age Bias Costs Us All."

Chapter 2

Age-Friendly Communities

We become agents of change.

Jane King
Alexandria, Virginia AARP volunteer

In August 2019, U.S. Senator Gary Peters (D-MI) got on his motorcycle for his fourth annual tour of his home state. Peters was and is an avid motorcycle rider who founded the bipartisan Senate Motorcycle Caucus in 2017, making his mode of transportation not that bizarre. Over the course of the five-day trip, with stops planned in Metro Detroit, Flint, the Upper Peninsula, Traverse City, Grand Rapids, and Mid-Michigan, Peters discussed issues that were important to the state. Not surprisingly, the usual senatorial subjects—jobs, economic growth, environmental protection, and national defense—formed the substance of Peters's conversations with Michiganers.[1]

On the third day of the 2019 tour, before moving on to Traverse City, Peters made a point of stopping his bike at the Ishpeming Senior Citizens Center. There he met with some residents of the Upper Peninsula town (population 6,470), focusing on his efforts to help set national standards for creating age-friendly communities. "I will continue working in a bipartisan manner to ensure that age-friendly communities keep expanding across Michigan," Peters said, a reference to the legislation he had recently introduced with Senator John Boozman (R-AR) to amend LBJ's Great Society–era Older Americans Act of 1965 (the first federal-level initiative aimed at providing comprehensive services for older adults). If passed, the amendment would require departments across the federal government to develop a national set of goals on healthy aging and age-friendly communities. The new set of standards would also support aging in place and senior access to preventive and long-term care, including home- and community-based health services and caregivers.[2]

While Senator Peters's motorized barnstorming was classic political maneuvering, it symbolized something major, even historic, taking place within our society. By the summer of 2019, the idea and practice of age-friendly communities had come a long way, a result of global, national, and local initiatives launched over the course of the past decade. Peters's brief visit to the Ishpeming Senior Citizens Center may have seemed relatively insignificant within the big scheme of things, but it was prime evidence of sweeping change that was doing nothing less than remaking the cultural landscape of America.

A Silver Tsunami

As editors Tine Buffel, Sophie Handler, and Chris Phillipson made clear in their *Age-Friendly Cities and Communities: A Global Perspective*, the subject of age-friendly communities is exceptionally multi- and interdisciplinary. Scholars and practitioners in a wide variety of fields, including social gerontology, social policy, housing, public health, urban studies, sociology, and geography, are likely to have some interest in the subject, as do policymakers, urban planners, international organizations, and service providers. Older people have a vested interest in making life age friendlier for themselves and others, of course, but it becomes evident in the following pages that all of us can benefit from making places age inclusive. As its subtitle makes clear, *Age-Friendly Cities and Communities* leaves no doubt that the age-friendly movement is a global phenomenon, with at least as much attention devoted to the subject in Europe and Asia as in the United States.[3]

In another recently published collection of essays dedicated to age-friendly communities around the world, *The Global Age-Friendly Community Movement: A Critical Appraisal*, editor Philip B. Stafford (an anthropologist) dates the beginning of the movement in the United States to 2003. That first effort, the AdvantAge Initiative, was a nationwide community development project of the Center for Home Care Policy and Research. The project broke down an age-friendly community into four domains based on findings from a series of focus groups. In addition to AARP, which is much discussed in this chapter, other major national organizations, including the National Association of Area Agencies on Aging, the Environmental, the Centers for Disease Control and Prevention, Grantmakers in Aging, and the Administration on Aging, all devoted energy to the movement in their own way, laying the foundation for bigger things to come.[4]

In my own book *Aging in America: A Cultural History*, I locate the real beginnings of the age-friendly movement in the United States to Douglas County, Colorado, in 2007. Like many areas across the country, Douglas County had long been a desired spot for young families to put down roots. In 2007, however, local leaders and state legislators began to notice a pronounced demographic shift taking place in the county and surrounding areas. The over-60 population in the county was growing and would continue to grow at an alarmingly fast rate—nearly 60% between 2004 and 2009—with other counties in Colorado also experiencing a spike in the percentage of older residents. "We're looking at a silver tsunami," said Lafayette City (in Boulder County) councilman Jay Ruggerri, foreseeing a greater need for services for the aging such as meals for shut-ins, medical aid, and transportation.[5]

Something very different was taking place in the suburbs of Denver, however. In that city, schools and recreation facilities for children were being built at a cost of hundreds of millions of dollars, with no such "silver tsunami" taking place there. Two very different kinds of communities—one relatively old and one relatively young—were simultaneously emerging in Colorado. State senators, especially those on the legislature's Joint Budget Committee, could see a tug of war over public funding coming as each kind of community lobbied for resources. "You never want to be in a place where you have to vote for taking care of old people or vote for educating young people," said Senator Abel Tapia, a Democrat from Pueblo, "but that's where we'll be."[6]

As the "silver tsunami" approached the nation's shores and raised questions about how taxpayers' money should be spent, significantly more attention was beginning to be paid to the aging of America. The oldest baby boomers were beginning to turn 60 in the first decade of the 21st century, sparking an increasingly loud conversation about how they might choose to spend their remaining decades. Because of boomers' numbers and influence, their third act of life presented major consequences to the social, economic, and political interests of the country. While many worried about an impending "aging crisis" due to a lack of financial and health-care resources, others focused on how boomers could continue to grow as individuals and contribute to society. Discovering a "cure" for aging remained a hot pursuit, however, this despite more research showing that getting older was not the debilitating process many Americans believed it to be. As the battle between the anti-aging community and its foes intensified, so did the effort by marketers to offer innovative products and services dedicated to older consumers. The age wave was now an incoming tide and something that could no longer be ignored.

Concern about an aging population was hardly limited to a handful of counties in Colorado. The cultural geography of the nation as a whole was in transition as the demographic makeup of suburbs gradually became older. "Suburbs, which previously were considered youthful and family-friendly parts of America, will . . . become a fast-graying part of our national landscape," noted William Frey in a report released by the Brookings Institution in 2007. With the number of seniors expected to grow at a rate of nearly 36% over the following decade (four times faster than the nation as a whole), demographers like Frey were urging community leaders to start planning for the population shift. Given the history of the country over the past half-century, seniors outnumbering children in the suburbs was, for many local politicians, an understandably difficult concept to accept, making the planning process a slow one. The suburbs of Atlanta, Washington, and Dallas were aging particularly fast, however, with Chicago and Los Angeles soon to follow the trend.[7]

It was a surprise to many that it was the suburbs of major cities rather than traditional areas of retirement in states such as Florida and Arizona that were rapidly aging. The fact was, however, that the common perception that massive hordes of older people continually moved to warm places after retiring was now wrong. Fewer than 2% of those between the ages of 55 and 64 moved across state lines each year, another study by the Brookings Institution found, with the number even lower for people older than 65. Contrary to popular belief, older people simply didn't move that much, making it highly probable that baby boomers would "age in place," i.e., stay in their current homes. The idea of leaving an expensive-to-heat house in the snowy north for a condo where it was endless summer was perhaps an appealing one, but the reality of retirees staying put made more sense. Many boomers grew up in the suburbs, became urbanites as young singles, and then moved back to the burbs after marrying and raising kids, making the prospect of relocating to an unfamiliar community that was hundreds or thousands of miles away not particularly attractive. In short, boomers were much more likely to remain in their houses or possibly move across town to more affordable, senior-friendly homes than head south after working full time.[8]

Although there was considerable variance based on local demographics, a good number of communities in the United States had begun to address in some degree the growing wave of aging residents. Baltimore was being looked to as a model of proactive planning in this regard. Community leaders, led by John P. Stewart, executive director of the city's Commission on Aging and Retirement Education (CARE), were determined to create what they considered nothing less than "a reinvented society." (Part of it likely had to do with the hometown Baltimore Longitudinal Study, which was still going strong as it neared its own half-century mark.)[9] "We're trying to create a blueprint for the design of an elder-friendly city which, when you come right down to it, will be a citizen-friendly city," Stewart told the editor in chief of *Nursing Homes/Long Term Care Management* in a 2006 interview. Developing sufficient resources for health care, transportation, public safety, job opportunities, and continuing education were all ways in which neighborhoods in Baltimore would be improved, he held, and not just for seniors but for everyone. Thirty-eight percent of the city's home-owners were more than 60 years old, making CARE's biggest priority to make it possible for those residents to "age in place" should they wish as they got older.[10]

It's important to note that while age friendliness is undoubtedly a critical issue, both now and in the future, poverty is an even more serious one. Many older adults are dependent on Social Security and Medicaid, which means having to live on a relatively low fixed income. High medical bills can wreak havoc with anyone's budget, especially those unable to afford supplemental health insurance. Making communities age friendly is a more than worthwhile endeavor but addressing the nation's high poverty rate among the aged is crucial when considering ways to make the lives of older people better. Ideally, poverty will become a greater component within the concept of age-friendly communities as the movement continues to evolve.

The Age of Aging

The aging of not just the United States but much of the world is the result of a perfect storm of factors centered on health care and demographics. Longer lon-gevity, improved health care, and the life span arc of baby boomers are the major reasons why more than 20% of the world's population will be age 65 or more by 2030. Baby boomers' leanings to keep working as long as possible and age in place are also helping to change the dynamics of aging. (In a 2012 study for the National Council of Aging, 90% of older adults surveyed said they planned to stay in their homes in their later years.)[11] Just as they initially rejected their parents' model of consumer capitalism in their youth, so are many boomers now largely rejecting their parents' model of retirement. Moving to a 55+ condo in a warm, sunny place (think of the hilarious "Del Boca Vista" episode of *Seinfeld*) just doesn't have the same appeal for boomers. The classic model of retirement living for those who could afford it—a car-dependent gated subdivision with cookie-cutter homes, perhaps on a golf course—is simply not the way the coun-tercultural generation wants to spend its third act of life.[12]

Assisted living centers and nursing homes are understandably perceived as an even worse option. Staying put in one's own community and in the same home where one has raised a family or downsizing to a nearby apartment is now a common goal among many boomers. (Being close to the grandkids is another key motivation to not seek greener pastures.) It is thus in the interest of all communities—not just those dedicated to older adults—to be age friendly in order to retain their current residents and best serve their needs.

The graying of America and the world has over the past decade deeply shaped the thinking behind community planning. Traditionally, planners focused on two areas—businesses and housing—with economic and residential concerns top of mind. The presence or likelihood of a larger percentage of older citizens has broadened this basic "earn-and-spend" view of how civic leaders can best plan for community life. Now many planners see their respective communities in terms of the built environment (primarily housing and transportation) and the social environment (primarily recreation and civic engagement). Along with this wider lens has come a greater understanding that the latter category, while less costly, is just as important as the former. Social engagement is a community's lifeblood, after all, the heart and soul of what makes a small town or big city a good place to live. The onset of our "age of aging" is heavily responsible for this positive revisioning of the DNA of community life.[13]

Both the WHO and the United Nations have taken serious note of this unprecedented phenomenon of global aging by launching programs and policies designed to stem the many potential challenges it presents. Many communities in this country and others are simply not prepared for the presence and needs of thousands or millions of septuagenarians, octogenarians, and nonagenarians. The common vision of a more age-friendly world in which the well-being of older people is being actively addressed is a sure sign that we are moving in the right direction, however. Since 2010, WHO has ambitiously and wisely designated certain cities and counties around the world as worthy of belonging to its Global Network of Age-friendly Communities and Cities. The network offers a research-based blueprint or roadmap for cities and countries to follow, something many places have done. WHO leadership believed that two global trends in particular—aging and urbanization—had to be formally addressed lest millions of lives be negatively affected over the next few decades. Through its network, communities have the very real opportunity to, as the saying goes, "Think globally, act locally."

Within the United States, WHO's effort is led by AARP, the country's leading advocate for the aging population. With a membership of about 40 million and a media empire consisting of a magazine (the largest circulation of any), bulletin, radio and television programming, and website, the nonprofit and nonpartisan organization has enormous power. (AARP members would represent the third-largest economy in the world if they were a country.) Since 2012, hundreds of American cities and counties have applied to AARP's Age-Friendly Network in order to be recognized as age friendly. Included in each application is an outline of what steps will be taken to make their community a more attractive place for older people to live (or just visit). Enlisting in the program is a five-year commitment that begins with assessing the needs of older residents (50-plus), forming a plan, putting it in place, and then determining how well it works.[14]

Rather than be considered an end, however, a community being designated as age friendly is more the beginning. Membership in the network means elected officials have made the commitment to actively work toward making their community a good place for people of all ages, not that the town, city, county, or state is currently age friendly or a good place to retire. In that sense, the network is aspirational—a philosophy that contrasts the stringent outcome-based approach to which most local governments adhere. The good news is that initiatives begun in a municipality often spread throughout a county like kudzu, with entire states recently jumping on board as governors see the demographic writing on the wall.

Joining the growing movement, which includes all shapes and sizes of communities, including rural areas, takes some doing. There are eight areas or domains to consider when seeking the AARP Network's designation: outdoor spaces and buildings, transportation, housing, social participation, respect and social inclusion, civic participation and employment, communication and information, and community and health services. The range of questions for applicants to ask themselves is rather mind-boggling, combining the macro and the micro. Is there enough affordable housing? If not, do zoning laws have to be changed? Can older people easily navigate the public parks? Are there holding bars in public bathrooms? Are there benches along heavily walked sidewalks or nature trails? Is there enough public transportation, taxis, and Ubers? Do the "Walk" signs blink long enough for everyone to get across wider streets? Most important, would people want to grow old here?[15]

The local network chapter to which I belong, the Miami-Dade County Age-Friendly Initiative, serves as a good example of the kinds of activities taking place in this country and around the world. Members consider age friendliness relative to both the built environment and the social environment by thinking about how residents engage within physical spaces and through relationships with other people. Communities and health systems are deeply intertwined, with each of those shaped by governmental and institutional policies. (With many lives at stake, the COVID-19 pandemic strengthened those connections.) The county works closely with each of the cities that have been designated age friendly, helping them develop action plans and encouraging them to focus their efforts because of limited resources. AARP serves as a liaison or facilitator, connecting local initiatives with state or national programs to share information and resources. As a bonus, my local chapter, like many others, offers "mini-grants"— relatively small but very useful funds to an individual or group developing or trying to grow a program designed to help older adults in some way.

Part of the idea behind age-friendly communities has to do with the fact that people tend to stay in communities longer than they expected. All kinds of changes are likely to take place within a household over the course of decades—income often fluctuates, kids move out (and back in!), and health problems typically come with age. The perfect house in the perfect neighborhood in the perfect city at age 30 may be less than perfect at age 60, the reason why communities should adjust to the different needs of people across the age spectrum. Things typically not considered important while raising a family—good access to public transportation and more affordable housing options, say—can become quite important if one wants to age in place. "Communities should seek to have the options that people want and need to stay and thrive in the neighborhood and setting of their choice," wrote Rodney Harrell of AARP in *Aging Today* in 2019, thinking that "every community should strive to meet a goal of being livable for all residents, whatever their age."[16]

The desire for a community to become age friendly is often a great opportunity for the public and private sectors to work together on a common goal. Planning commissions in a city or region might reach out to local businesses to come up with a strategic plan that outlines ways to keep younger people from moving away and to help older citizens with the typical challenges that come with aging. Local chambers of commerce and economic development agencies are also likely to get into the mix, with the state's AARP representative to guide the process. Opportunities for improvement are detailed, as are best practices based on case studies, with strategies and associated costs then included in the plan.[17]

Completion of the five-year, age-friendly community process is naturally a good time for local leaders to assess accomplishments to date and to determine what else should be done to make a city or county an even better place for people of all ages to live. In 2020, Columbus, Ohio, along with Franklin County, did just that after what elected officials in each described as "five years of robust discovery and innovation with older adult residents and those who serve them." Quite a number of surveys, focus groups, and walk audits were completed; thousands of emergency preparedness kits were distributed; presentations were made to more than 10,000 people; pilot programs in both transportation and housing were launched; and a ton of written material documenting the initiative was produced, all of this in addition to the usual advocacy for aging that was part of the political scene.[18]

Those kinds of efforts were well beyond the needs and capabilities of small towns in rural areas that recognize the value of becoming age-friendlier communities. In such areas, no research-based strategic plan is called for; instead, more modest but still important changes are put into play. In Sullivan, Maine (population 1,200), for example, there was no talk of building a new senior center, enhancing the towns' parks, adding transit routes, or coming up with housing solutions for the older population. Rather, it was things like building a community garden, recruiting people to serve on community boards, and conceiving a wellness fair, all things that promised to develop and maintain social connections. (Maine gets mighty cold in the winter, often leading to social isolation.) Without the dollars that an urban government can have, small towns rely on volunteers to get the work done and even passing the hat when funds need to be raised. These days, phrases like "investing in social sustainability," "fostering community," and "strengthening the safety net" are just as likely to be heard in a meeting in a small town as in a big city. Alexandria, Minnesota; Carlsbad, New Mexico; and Jackson Hole, Wyoming, are other towns that have put age-friendly initiatives in place despite having relatively small populations and low budgets.[19]

Livability for All

Elected officials interested in having their communities designated age friendly by investing, fostering, and strengthening more often than not have much work ahead of them. Hired consultants, nonprofit representatives, volunteer advisors, and other key stakeholders, such as business and faith leaders as well as academics, are typically brought into the process in order to achieve "economies of scope," i.e., efficiencies and synergies to be gained by addressing multiple enterprises at the same time. A mayoral advisory council may very well be formed to chart out a course based on AARP's guidelines, with the state's attorney general sometimes invited to the proceedings. Input from teenage residents is often solicited, especially as related to recreational activities, library policies, and environmental action.

Rather than be a one-size-fits-all plan, however, AARP's initiative is a framework to be customized based on a community's unique characteristics. While the platform is consistent, local communities are apt to come up with some interesting twists. In Sausalito, for example, the city passed regulations offering older homeowners exemptions from permit fees when making home modifications that increase accessibility.[20] (This despite the fact that most of those planning to age in place don't believe extensive and expensive modifications to their homes will be necessary.) Communities take the time required to ensure that the initiative is done right versus fast; it's not unusual to complete a year-long research and assessment phase followed by a year-long strategic planning phase before moving to the implementation phase of the five-year project.

Creating a narrative based on the community's historic and cultural attributes is vital for buy-in among the many disparate parties involved. (Some communities are creating a Hall of Fame to commemorate local heroes, past and present.) Cross-pollination—exchanging ideas and responsibilities among the various team members—is an excellent way to gain consensus and move things forward. Diversity and inclusion are prioritized (issues related to race, gender, and sexual orientation are typically addressed), and translators are sought for those who don't speak English. Most important, perhaps, an intergenerational approach—what is sometimes called "livability for all"—is employed in order to make it clear that the effort goes well beyond the benefit of the older population. Everyone is aging all the time, of course, making initiatives universal in scope (and difficult to challenge based on an argument of special interest).[21]

A community's journey toward age friendliness often takes interesting twists and turns, especially with regard to intergenerationality. Sometimes older adults are paired with children in creative ways to bridge constructed barriers. Reading a book or working on an art project together, for example, is an opportunity for people of vastly different ages to connect on a personal level. For some reasons on which we can speculate, there's a special connection between young and old people; grandparents and grandchildren and those of their respective ages often form a powerful bond that is different from that between parents and children. Such creative exercises are thus likely to prove intellectually and emotionally beneficial for all parties. More progressive age-friendly communities are apt to make a dedicated effort to foster a mutually beneficial relationship between older adults and kids. Students are sometimes asked to write about the role of an older person in their lives, for instance, with these essays then shared (and judged!) by patrons of senior centers (which are increasingly being renamed "intergenerational centers"). High schoolers have recorded the histories of older citizens in their community, another great example of bridging the age gap. Murals are being painted by people of all ages, with diversity often the chosen theme.[22]

Getting young and old people together can go well beyond seeding age friendliness in a particular community. There is good reason to believe that intergenerational mingling can have long-lasting benefits on a society-wide level, a very good thing given the age segregation that exists in the United States. Based on his research, Cornell University professor Karl Pillemer made the rather startling claim that contemporary America was "the most age-segregated society that's ever been," the result of many different and divisive decisions made in education, work, and housing over the course of a century. For Marc Freedman and Trent Stamp, this lack of contact between generations has bred "widespread ageism rooted in stereotypes," making it in our best interests to find more ways to embed intergenerationality into age-friendly initiatives.[23] One interesting activity funded by a mini-grant from the Miami-Dade County Age Friendly Initiative was Mind&Melody, an interactive music program that put seniors and kids together, a great example of local intergenerationality.

Intergenerational exchanges are especially important when it comes to technology. College students are known to volunteer time to show more technology-challenged folks how to use that cellphone, computer, or tablet or download an app.[24] Needs vary dramatically based on the individual and the fact that there are the "young-old" (say 65 years old) and the "old-old" (85 and up). The latter group tends to be less technologically fluent and, given the ever-growing need to do things online, considerable effort is being made to assist the digitally challenged. At the same time, communities are making it possible for residents to register for events and access information in an analog way—i.e., telephone or print—should they choose to do so.[25]

Active Senior Living

The two megatrends that stirred WHO to develop its age-friendly program—aging and urbanization—are often woven together. A fusion of these major societal shifts can be seen in the "empty nester" phenomenon that is taking place in many cities in the United States. A good number of older couples from the suburbs are selling their larger homes and moving into apartments in urban areas to take advantage of all the amenities of city life. Letting go of all the upkeep that comes with house ownership is another reason to head downtown. While de-suburbanization skews toward the wealthy and leans toward trendier neighborhoods, there isn't any reason why most of those whose kids have (finally) flew the nest can't be part of it. Mixed-income developments can be found in or near many downtown areas, making this migration an important one relative to age friendliness.

Urban communities are indeed responding to the desire for some baby boomers to get out of the 'burbs (much like they wanted to in their youth) by creating opportunities for them to stay connected and healthy. Walkability—the possibility to make one's way to restaurants, museums, and, importantly, doctor's offices without driving—is one of the primary selling points for cities interested in attracting older adults.[26] From this perspective, it can be said that the principles of new urbanism—the planning and development approach in which walkability is prioritized—ideally dovetail with those of age friendliness. At least one study found that walkable, mixed-use neighborhoods are not just convenient but can promote wellness among older adults. "We found that, despite declining physical function, older adults report greater independence in instrumental activities when they live in environments with more land-use diversity," researchers Philippa Clarke and Linda K. George wrote in the *American Journal of Public Health*, findings that nicely align with age-friendly communities' focus on the built environment.[27]

The ascent of age friendliness poses major consequences for the nation's population distribution. Sun City and other retirement communities used to define the good life for older Americans, but baby boomers want to live among people of all ages and cultural orientations rather than just people who look and act a lot like them. Because they do not resemble real life (and are decidedly uncool), communities restricted to those 55+ and designed for "active senior living" are not well positioned to be considered age friendly regardless of the services offered or improvements made to their infrastructure. Boomers love authenticity, diversity, and energy and are thus choosing places to live that incorporate those values. As well, the idea of sorting communities into buckets defined by age—i.e., "young, "middle-aged," and "old"—is a dated concept. No one, especially your typical baby boomer, suddenly gets "old" when he or she turns a certain age, making any product or service purposely conceived to fit the wants or needs of an older consumer probably a bad idea.[28]

One might not think hipster neighborhoods would be a destination of choice for people who were eligible to vote in the 1968 presidential election, but such is the case. With cash in hand, wealthier boomers are moving into trendy urban neighborhoods like Williamsburg in Brooklyn, attracted to the place for the same, simple reason many 20-somethings love it—it's interesting and inspiring. Developers of high-rise, high-end condos in that part of New York City have been somewhat surprised that not every buyer is a millennial making big bucks or with a fat bank account courtesy of mommy or daddy. Rather, it's mommy and/or daddy herself or himself that wants in, with these 50- or 60-somethings elated to live somewhere that exudes such *joie de vivre*. Many of these boomers are relocating from the family-friendly suburbs, finding hipstervilles to be a wonderful change of pace from the house and town that served them very well while they were raising kids. Uber-cool downtown Seattle, artsy LoHi (Lower Highlands) in Denver, and the Rittenhouse Square area of Philadelphia are also experiencing an influx of boomers, making savvy developers like Toll Brothers take note and create a "city living" division. Younger homeowners may not be particularly happy about people who look disturbingly like their mom or dad establishing digs in their hood but should find consolation in the fact that their apartment is probably now worth a lot more money. It's in the best interests of such communities to bake in age friendliness into their cultural geography to keep attracting older residents.[29]

Other baby boomers, however, are going the opposite way by leaving big cities for smaller, more manageable towns. Ironically, perhaps, it can be easier to make friends in communities with lower populations, if only for the simple reason that there's a greater chance of bumping into the same people. College towns hold special appeal for those thinking of relocating to a place offering considerable intergenerational mixing. With loads of young, mostly enthusiastic people looking forward rather than backward, such towns represent a more diverse alternative to a traditional retirement community. There's a palpable sense of energy on and around college campuses, with the always exciting aura of learning in the air. Boomers are returning to such communities for the intellectual stimulation and cultural amenities, especially those in which they may have lived 40 or 50 years ago when they were students. Fully aware of this, civic leaders are aggressively seeking to be deemed age friendly while also flaunting free or low-cost classes, regular sporting events, concerts, and lectures for those 55+. Many such towns, including Ann Arbor (University of Michigan), Austin (University of Texas), Oxford (Ole Miss), and Cambridge (Harvard and MIT), offer good health care, affordable housing, and are in states that are tax friendly to those with financial assets but relatively low incomes, increasing their age-friendly quotient.[30]

10,000 Americans

If nothing else, many communities find, going through the AARP's network process is a good exercise, revealing both strengths and weaknesses within the arena of age inclusivity. Committing to realize age-friendly status often prompts a community to complete desirable projects that were for some reason—usually funding—put on the back burner. AARP's website includes a Livability Index that makes it possible to see how a particular community measures up compared with others on a wide range of metrics and policies, which are then aggregated into a single score. Getting input from local residents is key not just to generate ideas but also to forge a mini-movement within the movement. Seeing a community through the lens of age friendliness leads to a deeper and richer understanding of what makes that place tick. One thing that becomes instantly clear is that there is a direct connection between livability and the built environment, an obvious but often overlooked relationship that heavily shapes residents' relative level of happiness.

Although the goal usually is to join the network, it also serves as a central rallying point around which to address issues related to an aging population. Advocacy becomes easier and perhaps more effective when it is channeled into a single directive. Deciding to become certified or even exploring the possibility of doing so is by default making a commitment to the well-being of older individuals and, in a grander sense, striving to make the country and the world better places. The initial research phase generates valuable input that feeds directly into a plan of action. Surveys and questionnaires are often sent not just to older residents but to middle-aged adults who in a decade or two will qualify for "senior" status, and focus groups are occasionally held to further probe relevant issues. "What services are missing from the community?" researchers ask, with this information used to inform the local age-friendly initiative.

The steps required to even have a chance of joining the network can in larger cities cost millions or even billions of dollars (but just thousands in small towns and rural areas). Funding for AARP's network sometimes replaces dollars that have been cut by other nonprofits, such as United Way. AARP's program is sometimes integrated within existing, related projects, usually those addressing health or transportation issues. If big money is at stake, a proposition is often presented as a ballot issue (lobbied by an AARP state chapter), allowing voters to decide if their taxes should be spent in such a way. Raising the sales tax on a relevant line item (such as transportation) is frequently the means to raise money. Not surprisingly, older voters turn out in droves to support the resolution, sometimes making the difference in whether or not it will be passed. Happily, the changes made to a community's physical infrastructure end up benefiting not just older folks but everyone. Businesses that have complied with the standards sometimes display window stickers as a sign of age friendliness (not unlike the ubiquitous rainbow gay-friendly sticker).

The widely disseminated media factoid of "10,000 Americans Are Turning 65-years-old Every Day" is itself enough for community leaders to think long and hard about age friendliness. Expectedly, that national figure directly translates to population forecasts in local towns, cities, and counties, often quite alarmingly. Atlanta's 65-plus population, for example, is likely to nearly triple by 2040 and, in many places, the number of people over 80 is projected to double over the next decade or two. Already in some communities, a third of residents are 55 years old or older, and they will obviously all get continually older unless or until they die. Such figures are something that makes city planners and managers who are attentive to sustainability take notice and green-light modifications to existing resources. Some classrooms at community centers previously used for children's daycare are being reconfigured as spaces for older adults to spend time, for example, an indicator of the sea change taking place in the nation's population. The number of Americans aged 65 or older will eclipse the school-age population (5–17) in 2034, according to the U.S. Census Bureau, another statistic that is serving as a catalyst for change.[31]

For years, it should be noted, many city or county governments across the country were resistant to aging advocates' pleas to make local communities more age friendly. That has changed dramatically over the past decade as civic leaders recognize not just the need but also the opportunity to invest in programs designed to improve the quality of life for older citizens. Beyond rethinking how taxpayers' money should be spent (foundations and private philanthropists also often kick in some grant money), there is an economic incentive for elected officials to make their respective community age friendly. The prospect of hundreds or thousands of current or new residents with nest eggs to spend is the stuff of a mayor's dreams, with he or she fully aware that such a thing could also bring more businesses to provide services for these citizens. Many communities have seen their younger adults go to big cities for college or greater job opportunities, making the presence of a significant number of financially comfortable older adults a highly attractive one.[32]

It's Not about Leaves

With its mission to serve the interests of older Americans, AARP is without a doubt in the bullseye of age friendliness in the United States. Helping create age-friendly communities is arguably AARP's most important endeavor, and the organization devotes a tremendous amount of effort at the national, state, and local levels in this regard. People are deployed and materials distributed to promote the idea and practice of age friendliness, all of this backed up by a powerful (some might say propagandist) media campaign. While AARP provides local community leaders with free resources to plan for their aging populations, even an organization as large and powerful as it recognizes that it can't do it alone. Other organizations, such as the International City-County Management Association, may enlist in the cause, and YMCAs, with their focus on physical activity and socializing, also tend to make great partners. Complementary relationships blossom in such collaborations, frequently creating synergistic outcomes.[33]

"Access" is a word often heard in age-friendly initiatives, whether that means providing free Internet, caregiving services, or wellness clinics. Special attention is paid to ability, specifically if public spaces can be used by those with some physical constraints. As well, the interests of pedestrians are elevated, framing age friendliness within the context of new urbanism. Adding more lighting and signage are other ways communities are paying more attention to the interests and safety of pedestrians, a very good thing as ever-more motorized transportation devices appear on our streets and, more troubling, sidewalks. Because the possibilities for a community to demonstrate age friendliness are literally endless—ranging from library book delivery to a subsidized handyman service to any number of other conveniences—priorities have to be set. Most important, perhaps, is communication (both online and print), as many residents simply don't know what existing services are available.

Expectedly, given their role, much thought is assigned to senior centers when charting a course of age friendliness. These buildings or campuses typically serve as the principal gathering spot for a community's older residents and thus play an integral part in the group's physical and mental well-being. It has been well documented that some kind of social interaction is key to health and longevity, and senior centers are in an ideal position to support that critical function. Classes and programs in everything from self-esteem to money management to tai chi to indoor rock climbing (seriously!) are often given in these town halls, with the opportunity to see old friends and meet new people, which is as important as the material to be learned or activity to be pursued. Ensuring that a senior center is conveniently located and accessible is a major concern among city planners seeking to join ARRP's network.

Group efforts are where local AARP initiatives really shine. In the spirit of a Habitat for Humanity home-building project (inspired perhaps by an Amish barn raising), local volunteers sometimes get together to make a specific part of their community more age friendly. In Fort Worth in 2018, for example, volunteers painted curbs and crosswalks to make the Linwood neighborhood safer for pedestrians and created a makeshift traffic circle to slow down vehicles in that section of town. Before doing the actual work, volunteers, many of them now retired, typically walk through an area to spot potential problems. Walking audits are commonly considered the only real way to get the literal lay of the land, although it's already known in which spots there is a history of problems, such as pedestrian or bicycle accidents. Neighborhoods with a senior housing complex get special attention, with improving mobility for older folks typically the priority. American sidewalks are frequently in rough shape, we learn from AARP stories reporting progress being made by age-friendly community initiatives, and cars—moving and parked—are an enemy. (Moms and dads pushing strollers face the same hazards as older people, it should be noted, a good example of how improvements to the built environment are inherently intergenerational in scope.) "We demonstrated how really small changes can make a huge impact," said Melodia Gutierrez, AARP Texas outreach and advocacy director after the few days of effort in Fort Worth.[34]

Age-friendly initiatives can be reminiscent of an America that one might think is long gone or existed only in Norman Rockwell artwork. Also in 2018, over a hundred volunteers scattered through the Milwaukee suburb of Shorewood to clean up the yards of dozens of older residents. With winter approaching, members of churches, scout groups, and the education community raked leaves and found places for outdoor furniture. While important in its assigned purpose, the cleanup served as a means to seed the bigger idea of age friendliness. "It's not about leaves," explained Sue Kelley, the facilitator of Shorewood Connects, which started the project a decade earlier, adding, "it's about connections and relationships." Age-friendly communities like Shorewood recognize that older residents contribute in valuable ways, making them an asset versus a liability.[35]

Urban planners often are a key part of a team effort grounded in making communities age inclusive. Age-friendly community initiatives encompass a broad spectrum of basic infrastructural components, including housing, public transit, and access to services. Successfully aging in place, social interaction, and safety are the common goals. Working with city departments is essential;

putting up more stop signs, for example, can entail a massive amount of bureaucratic red tape. Because they by necessity bring people together for a common cause, grassroots programs tend to strengthen ties within a neighborhood, this itself making a community more age friendly. That it is ordinary citizens doing much of the work is another important piece in the larger scheme of revitalizing civic and public life.[36]

Because the United States is, when it comes to transportation, primarily a car culture, making it possible (and hopefully easy) for older residents to get around town represents a big chunk of age-friendly community efforts. Those of a certain age are known to not renew their driving licenses when it's time, often at the urging of relatives worried about the safety of their loved one (or that of another driver or pedestrian). Keeping a car is also expensive, and many older people living on a fixed income simply can't afford it. Providing some kind of alternative and affordable transportation is thus vital if a community is going to label itself truly age friendly. People who don't drive commonly fear going out at night lest they be stranded, something that magnifies the very real and quite terrible possibility of social isolation. (Depression and chronic illnesses like heart disease are tied to seclusion and loneliness.) Buses (which comply with the Americans with Disabilities Act) are good, but shuttle or trolley services are better, making a fleet of door-to-door "Dial-a-Rides" an important item in a budget. Subsidizing taxi fares is yet another option, and Uber and Lyft have emerged as popular ways to get from Point A to Point B and back without breaking the bank.[37]

The Place They Call Home

Any community being officially recognized as age friendly is cause for celebration. Once a town, city, county, or state is granted approval to be part of AARP's network, press releases are more often than not immediately and proudly generated (following a public ceremony celebrating the designation, often held at a senior center). "Cincinnati Joins AARP Network of Age-Friendly Communities," reads one 2018 headline, a good example of local boosterism. The releases make nice public relations, of course, but there is plenty of steak to the sizzle. As well, receiving an invitation to the network allows community leaders to learn what best practices others are taking to realize age friendliness. This sharing of information can offer invaluable insights based on experiences from places near and far.[38]

The swapping of success stories is a very valuable, often overlooked, part of local age-friendly initiatives. Exchanging ways to lessen the chance of slips and falls, for example, can literally save lives. Especially in northern communities, where snow and ice on the ground for months at a time is a fact of life, the fear of falling is pervasive. Fully aware that a slip or fall often leads to major decline in health and quite possibly death, many older adults are reluctant to leave their homes, making weather another contributing factor in social isolation. (COVID-19, of course, put an extra burden on older people in many ways and no doubt accelerated the chance of isolation. Some communities responded by making possible medical appointments by phone and by offering online meetings and courses in fitness and entertainment using Zoom or another audio or video conferencing platform.)

Local age-friendly groups have come up with and shared creative solutions to the problem of falls and limited mobility. In 2020, for example, South Portland, Maine, launched a "Sand Buckets for Seniors" program in which free five-pound buckets of sand (actually a sand-and-salt mix) were distributed to those who asked for one. Forty or 50 requests were expected but over 200 came in, with additional requests for refills. The program was a true community affair—firefighters kicked in some money, as they usually got the call after a fall, and Home Depot sold the buckets for half-price. "Sand Buckets for Seniors" was received as a perfect example of little-things-can-mean-a-lot and a welcome thing given the state's demographics. (Maine has the oldest median age in the United States.) A snow-shoveling service, manned by volunteers, was also made available. "Maine's success in establishing age-friendly initiatives is rooted in Yankee ingenuity, practicality and community spirit, and stepping in where state government action has been lacking in past years," a journalist for the *Portland Press Herald* noted.[39]

Given the abundance of such positive stories from across the country, it was clear that age-friendly communities in the United States were much more than a passing trend. As in other countries, hundreds of American communities from coast to coast and in all sizes had enlisted in the movement by investing time, energy, and money in place-specific initiatives. By 2020, the idea of an age-friendly community had reached a tipping point of sorts, emerging as a cause around which local citizens from many different backgrounds could come together with a common goal: making life better for people of all ages. Understanding the long-term implications of an older population, leaders of communities big and small have to their credit stepped up to the plate by reimagining what constitutes a sense of place. While the steps taken have been remarkably consistent, based on the eight domains cited within AARP's network guidelines, each community can be said to have packaged age friendliness in its own unique way. This is, at the risk of being jingoistic, is America at its best, offering a direct challenge to the usual rhetoric of divisiveness and hate.

AARP is clearly seizing the day by further leveraging its success to date. The organization is not content to simply reflect on its victories since launching its network in 2012, recognizing the opportunity to extend its mission in different ways. In New York City in 2018, for example, the organization's staff decided to direct its public policy efforts not just within the Department of Aging but also throughout the city's many government agencies. "Our hope is that when New York City tackles new projects—whether it's a new park or a street improvement or a new supermarket, city officials think about an older clientele and what their needs will be," stated Chris Widelo, AARP associate state director for New York City. After getting millions in city funding the previous year, the organization set its goals on receiving more assistance for unpaid family caregivers and working with the mayor and City Council on more affordable housing.[40]

Not surprisingly, after seeing the impressive traction being made to advance age friendliness in local communities and counties, state officials began pursuing their own initiatives and designations. A chase to see which state was the "age friendliest" can be said to have begun, with any official recognition suggesting as much flaunted in the media. In December 2018, New York State was designated the first Age-Friendly State in the nation by AARP, an achievement that was rather wordily embedded in the state's Health Across All Policies initiative.

New York's designation as the first Age-Friendly State in the nation will bring increased attention to the Health Across All Policies initiative and the State's consideration of the impact of State policies and procedures on environmental, economic, and social factors to influence the health and well-being of all residents, especially older adults,

Executive Order 190 clumsily read. In simpler terms, the concept of age friendliness could now be imported into any number or kind of governmental legislation in New York State, dramatically extending its reach and influence.[41]

New York's neighbor to the southwest was not to be outdone by Executive Order No. 190, however. In May 2019, Rep. Wayne DeAngelo and Rep. Herbert Conaway, both Democrats, urged all New Jersey counties and municipalities to commit to becoming age-friendly communities, something if achieved could perhaps put that state on top of the age-friendly heap. When presented in the state legislature's Health and Senior Services Committee, Assembly Resolution 246 received 11 "yeas" and 0 "nays" in the roll call, another statewide victory for age friendliness.[42]

Age friendliness is operating on the federal level as well. In May 2019, Sen. John Boozman, a Republican from Arkansas, joined Senator Gary Peters of Michigan to introduce legislation that would direct federal agencies to set national standards for healthy aging and creating age-friendly communities. The Age-Friendly Communities Act would amend the Older Americans Act of 1965 by requiring departments across the federal government to develop a national set of goals on healthy aging and age-friendly communities and establish a public-private coordinating body to provide recommendations and best practices for implementing those goals.[43] The act, which had support from many organizations, including AARP, the Leadership Council of Aging Organizations, the National Area Agencies on Aging, National Alliance for Caregiving, Meals on Wheels America, and the Alzheimer's Association, was passed in March 2020.[44]

Congressmen from both sides of the political fence were also joining forces to move ahead age friendliness on a national level. In October 2019, Rep. Charlie Crist (D-FL) and Rep. Steve Watkins (R-KA) cosponsored a congressional bill to amend the Older Americans Act to enhance age-friendly communities for older individuals. The act would refocus federal efforts supporting aging at home and the services that facilitate better health and greater social and civic participation, including public transportation, greater walkability, and leisure activities.[45] The bill (H.R. 4827), which was part of the Dignity in Aging bill (H.R. 4334), was referred to the House Committee on Education and Labor and passed on a voice vote. "I'm proud to have secured this win for Pinellas seniors and seniors everywhere," Crist's press release stated, adding, "seniors deserve the option of living out their golden years in the place they call home."[46] In a relatively short time, the emergence of age-friendly communities had redefined what constituted one's golden years, a reason to be optimistic about where this nation is headed as we all get older.

Notes

1 "Peters Announces Fourth Annual Motorcycle Tour Across Michigan," *Peters. senate.gov*, July 29, 2019.

2 "Motorcycle Tour Day 3: Peters Tours Senior Center, Highlights Efforts to Support Age-Friendly Communities in Ishpeming," *Targeted News Service*, August 13, 2019.

3 Tine Buffel, Sophie Handler, and Chris Phillipson, eds., *Age-Friendly Cities and Communities: A Global Perspective* (Bristol, UK: Policy, 2019).

4 Philip B. Stafford, ed., *The Global Age-Friendly Community Movement: A Critical Appraisal* (New York: Berghahn Books, 2018).

5 Joey Bunch, "A Silver Tsunami," *Denver Post*, June 11, 2007, A1.

6 "A Silver Tsunami."

7 David Peterson, "Burbs to Be Hit with Senior Boom," *Minneapolis Star Tribune*, June 12, 2007, 1A.

8 Jane Adler, "There's No Place Like Home for Aging Boomers," *Chicago Tribune*, December 24, 2006, 4.

9 "Study on Aging Reaches the Half-Century Mark," *Washington Post*, December 9, 2008, F2.

10 "Peering into the Future of Aging," *Nursing Homes/Long Term Care Management*, August 2006, 22.

11 ncoa.org.

12 John F. Wasik, "Choosing a Place to Settle Down in the Age of Fitbit," *New York Times*, October 15, 2016, B4.

13 "Planning for the Ages," *Business NH Magazine*, March 2019, 37.

14 Ray Huard, "As Population Ages, Communities Plan: Almost 1 in 4 State Residents Will Be 60 by 2030," *AARP Bulletin*, November 2016, 52a.

15 Richard M. Barron, "Age-Friendly Communities Effort Hopes to Improve Aging in Guilford," *News & Record* (Greensboro, NC), June 2, 2018.

16 Rodney Harrell, "Choosing the Right Community—A Quality of Life Issue," *Aging Today*, July/August 2019, 5.

17 "Age Appropriate," *New Hampshire Business Review*, January 19–February 1, 2018, 4.

18 Katie White, "Age Friendly Columbus Looks Back at its First 5 Years," *Next City. org.*, December 8, 2020.

19 Jeffrey Spivak, "Age-Friendly Rural Planning," *Planning*, December 2020, 26–30.

20 Matthew Pera, "Marin Age-Friendly Efforts Reshape Lives, Communities," *Marin Independent Journal*, November 26, 2018, A1.

21 Shannon Guzman and Aldea Douglas, "Livability for All," *Planning*, December 2015, 21–24; See Andrew L. Dannenberg, Howard Frumkin, and Richard Jackson, eds., *Making Healthy Places: Designing and Building for Health, Well-Being, and Sustainability* (Washington, DC: Island Press, 2011).

22 Sue Kelley and Chris Swartz, "Intergenerational Communities: How Shorewood, Wisconsin, Engages Residents of All Ages," *Public Management*, December 2014, 12.

23 Marc Freedman and Trent Stamp, "The U.S. Isn't Just Getting Older. It's Getting More Segregated by Age," *Harvard Business Review*, June 6, 2018, 3–4. See Freedman's excellent, *How to Live Forever: The Enduring Power of Connecting the Generations* (New York: PublicAffairs, 2018).

24 "Intergenerational Communities: How Shorewood, Wisconsin, Engages Residents of All Ages."

25 Kelley Bouchard, "South Portland Joins Growing Number of Grassroots Groups Helping Maine Seniors," *Portland Press Herald (ME)*, January 13, 2020.

26 "EDITORIAL: All Maine Communities Can Become Age-Friendly," *Portland Press Herald (ME)*, October 3, 2016.

27 Philippa Clarke and Linda K. George, "The Role of the Built Environment in the Disablement Process," *American Journal of Public Health*, November 2005, 95(11), 1933–1939.

28 Lawrence R. Samuel, *Boomers 3.0: Marketing to Baby Boomers in Their Third Act of Life* (Santa Barbara, CA: Praeger, 2017) 41.

29 *Boomers 3.0* 41–42.

30 *Boomers 3.0* 42–43.

31 "Older People Projected to Outnumber Children for First Time in U/S. History," March 13, 2018, Release Number CB18-41. census.gov.

32 "Age-Friendly Communities Effort Hopes to Improve Aging in Guilford."

33 "For Age-Friendly Communities," *Public Management*, March 2016, 5.

34 Thomas Korosec, "A Livable Goal: Even Small Changes Have Big Impact as Fort Worth Strives to Be Age-Friendly," *AARP Bulletin*, May 2018, 36w.

35 David Lewellen, "Age-Friendly Helps Everyone: Localities Look to Upgrade Services, Safety," *AARP Bulletin*, January–February 2018, 48x.

36 "A Livable Goal: Even Small Changes Have Big Impact as Fort Worth Strives to Be Age-Friendly."

37 "As Population Ages, Communities Plan: Almost 1 in 4 State Residents Will Be 60 by 2030."

38 "Cincinnati Joins AARP Network of Age-Friendly Communities," *PR Newswire US*, December 19, 2018.

39 "South Portland Joins Growing Number of Grassroots Groups Helping Maine Seniors."

40 Philip Lentz, "Message to Officials: Weigh Impact on Older Residents," *AARP Bulletin*, December 2017, 34n.

41 "United States: No. 190: Incorporating Health Across all Policies into State Agency Activities," *TendersInfo News*, December 14, 2018.

42 "New Jersey Assembly Resolution 246 Urges New Jersey Counties and Municipalities to Commit to Becoming Age-Friendly Communities. Reported Out of Assembly Committee, 2nd Reading," *US Official News*, May 21, 2019.

43 "Boozman, Peters Introduce Bipartisan Legislation to Support Healthy Aging and Age-Friendly Communities," *Targeted News Service*, May 22, 2019.

44 "Senate Passes Peters' Bipartisan Measures to Support Healthy Aging and Age-Friendly Communities," *States News Service*, March 4, 2020.

45 "H.R. 4827—To Amend the Older Americans Act of 1965 to Enhance Age-friendly Communities for Older Individuals," *US Official News*, October 24, 2019.

46 "Rep. Crist Issues Statement on Passage of Building Age-friendly Communities Act; ** Speech," *Targeted News Service*, October 29, 2019.

Chapter 3

Age-Friendly Work

Automation, artificial intelligence and other groundbreaking technologies might get top billing in conversations about the future of work, but as we live longer and healthier lives an increasingly multigenerational workforce will be just as transformative.

Forbes.com

Dear Savvy Senior: What resources can you recommend to help older job seekers? I'm 60 and have been out of work for nearly a year now. — *Seeking Employment*

Dear Seeking: While the U.S. job market has improved dramatically, challenges still persist. To help you find employment, there are job resource centers and online tools created for older job seekers.[1]

Many older adults likely found this March 2018 exchange in the *Honolulu Star-Advertiser* familiar territory. Jim Miller, the Savvy Senior columnist, proceeded to direct Seeking Employment and like-minded readers to a number of resources, including the American Job Center, the Senior Community Service Employment Program, AARP's Back to Work 50+ program, and job search sites like WhatsNext.com, RetiredBrains.com, RetirementJobs.com, Workforce50.com, and FlexJobs.com.[2]

While Miller's advice was certainly well-intentioned and perhaps helpful, the challenges facing 60-year-old Americans seeking employment were and remain mighty. Despite being unethical and illegal, ageism in the workplace is a fact of life and arguably the only arena in which discrimination is not just tolerated but also encouraged. "Young people are just smarter," Mark Zuckerberg (rather dumbly) said in 2007, a reflection of the age discrimination that

DOI: 10.4324/9781003196235-4   57

is so prevalent in the business community, especially within the tech industry. Older workers are a resource, not a burden, yet our current misperceptions—the legacy of decades-old thinking—is difficult to make go away. Today's 65-year-old looks, thinks, feels, and acts a lot different than the 1950s version, but the American workplace has yet to catch up with that fact. A society in which most older people are retired is a bad model to follow, and it's time we reject that for something different and better.

Keeping older employees in the workforce is a logical solution to many present and future economic and social problems, just one reason why a sea change in our attitudes and behaviors is much needed. In short, an age-friendly workplace offers our best opportunity to move older Americans to the asset side of the nation's balance sheet. Fortunately, this chapter shows, there are signs that age-friendly work may be becoming a feature of American life; if so, that is a very good thing that bodes well for the future of individuals, companies, and society as a whole.

I'm Not Done

In her 2016 *Overcoming Age Discrimination in Employment: An Essential Guide for Workers, Advocates & Employers*, Patricia G. Barnes, an attorney and former judge, did yeoman's work in showing how age discrimination in the workplace came to be an accepted and normal thing despite Congress passing the ADEA in 1967 (two years after the Older Americans Act). Designed "to promote employment of older persons based on their ability rather than age" and "to prohibit arbitrary age discrimination in employment," the act has proved to be a dismal failure. Because the act, unlike the much more legally robust Civil Rights Act of 1964, is essentially powerless and unenforceable, the hiring of people under the age of 40 has become the standard state of affairs (even within the federal government).[3] In her earlier book *Betrayed: The Legalization of Age Discrimination in the Workplace*, Barnes made the convincing case for Congress to scrap the ADEA and make age a protected class under Title VII of the Civil Rights Act of 1964, which currently prohibits employment discrimination based on race, religion, gender, and national origin.[4]

Patti Temple Rocks is somewhat more sanguine about the status of older people in the nation's workforce. In her *I'm Not Done: It's Time to Talk About Ageism in the Workplace*, the wonderfully named Rocks reminds us that things are a lot better than they were not that long ago in terms of equal opportunity, at least with regard to race and gender. As a middle-aged woman, Rocks worked at a large American company and had yet to experience any kind of bias. But after Rocks witnessed discrimination against a colleague who was in her early 50s at the time (the CEO labeled the woman "tired"), she became aware of how many older employees were being encouraged to leave or were pushed out because they were similarly fatigued. These employees, who were well paid because of their experience, were replaced by much cheaper younger workers, making Rocks conclude that ageism in the workplace was all about money. Then, inevitably, the same thing happened to her, leading to her decision to do what she could to stop what she called "this deeply hurtful and bad-for-business practice."[5]

In their book *The Talent Revolution: Longevity and the Future of Work*, Lisa Taylor and Fern Lebo focus on the gradual sidelining of baby boomers within the American workforce. In the 1980s and 1990s, boomers were undoubtedly an economic powerhouse, but now they are commonly seen as having little to contribute. With the rise of digital technology, baby boomers are often perceived by millennials as obsolete as a Betamax, Taylor and Lebo suggest, an unfair and untrue assessment. The authors see older adults as an essential component of the workplace of the future and longevity as paving the way to the coming "talent revolution." "We identify boomers as revolutionaries—a population of disruptors that is altering career patterns, creating new expectations, and demanding inclusion," they wrote, words that may come as a surprise to many in Corporate America.[6]

Chip Conley has come up with perhaps the most compelling scenario for older adults being welcomed in the workplace of the 21st century. The notion of modern elderhood has been simmering for some time, but Conley has shown how it could potentially serve as a platform for age-friendly work. In his early 50s, Conley sold his business and wasn't sure what to do next when he rather unexpectedly found a new gig as the designated "elder" for Airbnb, the online vacation rental marketplace. At that company, like most others that are tech-driven, digital intelligence has become the primary job qualification, putting young people with little managerial experience in major positions of power.

> Yet, at exactly the same time, there exists a generation of older workers with invaluable skills—high EQ (emotional intelligence), good judgement born out of decades of experience, specialized knowledge, and a vast network of contacts—who could pair with these ambitious millennials to create businesses that are built to endure,

Conley wrote in his *Wisdom at Work*. Conley advises older workers to repurpose their experience by seeking recognition as wise elders in organizations, not unlike how village elders in traditional societies wielded authority based on their wisdom that came with age.[7]

Yesterday's News

Conley offers full immersion in elderhood at his Modern Elder Academy (MEA), a luxury resort in Baja California Sur in El Pescadoro, Mexico. Participants share their stories of ageism, particularly as related to the workplace, and learn ways to integrate wisdom into their personal and professional lives. New Agey rituals like fire purges, talking sticks, healing sessions, coping workshops, oceanside yoga and meditation, and an on-call shaman (for blessing ceremonies) are part of the process of accepting the reality of getting older, even though a good number of attendees are only in their 30s and 40s. The one-week program costs $5,000 (room and board included), but that's a bargain for some of those from the highly paid, youth-obsessed tech industry. "We're all elders in the making," Conley said in 2019 soon after opening the doors of the MEA, which at that point had an average age of 52.[8]

A nice idea, certainly, but a quite ambitious one given how unfriendly the American workplace currently is to older people. For as long as it has existed, in fact, our corporate culture has been less than welcoming toward people of a certain age. Even in today's litigious climate, where lawyers are happy to take a case in which a company appears to have discriminated against a person based on a physical attribute, blatant, although hardly ever mentioned or acknowledged ageism is present in many, if not most, corporations. It's important to note that while big corporations are moving slow to end ageism in the workplace, if they are moving at all, small businesses, which fuel much economic growth in the United States, are more willing to employ older, experienced people, at least in leadership positions.

Unless he or she has an inside track, the odds of a baby boomer landing a managerial position as a new employee are long. Job applicants with college degrees from the 1970s and 1980s are typically promptly eliminated from consideration, even though they may be otherwise ideally qualified for a management position. If anything, one would expect people of different ages to be eagerly welcomed into organizations as a reflection of society, but this is simply not the case. The unfortunate truth is that discrimination against older people in the American workplace is commonplace (and illegal), a product of our deeply embedded cultural aversion to people considered past their prime. For a variety of reasons, young adults prefer to be around other younger adults, making age the only remaining demographic criterion in which it is acceptable to discriminate, often in the name of something like the completely nonsensical "overqualification."

Pervasive myths about older people have much to do with ageism in the workplace. Those in their third act of life are likely to be physically debilitated in some way, many think, or perhaps in cognitive decline. Having already lived "the best years of their lives," such folks are believed to be focused on the past and generally unhappy people. They are, additionally, deemed not curious and, worse, Luddites who are resistant to learning new things, especially in the digital world. In short, older workers—baby boomers, to be specific—are considered past their prime, over the hill, and yesterday's news, making the prospect of an intergenerational workforce impractical if not impossible.

Despite much evidence to the contrary, such untrue stereotypes are difficult to put behind us. The result of this kind of thinking has serious consequences, however, and runs against the grain of our democratic ideals. Ageism in the workplace is a shameful thing and not much different than the practices of previous generations of managers who would not hire qualified candidates if they happened to be African American or female. Human resources people's decision to define diversity in terms of skin color and gender but not by how many years a person has lived is bad not just for older people but also for companies. Research shows that older Americans often brin a valuable set of skills to any organization if only because they have more life experience.

The most logical way for the American workplace to become more age friendly is via the Diversity and Inclusion (D&I) movement. D&I is one of the primary initiatives in the corporate world, and it will no doubt continue to gain traction in the years ahead. Look at the managerial staffs of any major company and you will see people hired to ensure that workforces and boardrooms are fairly represented in terms of race, ethnicity, gender, and, ideally, physical ability and sexual orientation. A more advanced form of D&I recognizes and celebrates difference in terms of education, skill sets, experiences, knowledge, and even personalities.

Needless to say, this is a very good and long overdue thing that mostly came about because of the social, economic, and political pressures associated with the Black Lives Matter and MeToo movements. Sadly, corporations are resistant to change and will only do so if it serves their and their shareholders' financial interests. Formally establishing a D&I initiative makes sense for many reasons. Simply acknowledging that discrimination based on race, ethnicity, and gender exists and should be discouraged is a major achievement given the less than proud history of business in America and elsewhere. As important, perhaps, D&I is good for business. Embracing the reality that people are unique helps to fuel creativity and innovation, offering companies that do so a competitive edge, especially within the increasingly global marketplace. In short, a diverse and inclusive workforce improves the bottom line, making the initiative much more than good public relations. As with America itself, which was founded and continues to run on the principle of *e pluribus unum*—out of many, one— difference is good.

While age is in theory often part of a D&I initiative, it is rarely put into practice. Older workers are routinely and instantly rejected as job candidates by HR people and managers and encouraged to retire. Why is this so when many studies show that older people have a different kind of skill set that ideally complements companies' goals? Experience, perspective, and wisdom come with age, research has demonstrated, precisely what is needed for good short- and long-term decision-making. As with discrimination and bias based on race and gender, negative feelings about older people are deeply rooted and unlikely to change unless there is a social movement equivalent to Black Lives Matter and MeToo. Not just a multiracial, multiethnic, and multigender workforce but also a multigenerational workforce would be in the best interests of all kinds of organizations, however, and we should all work together to make that happen.

Unretirement

The importance of creating an age-friendly workplace has risen over the past decade or so as it became clear that the overwhelming majority of older workers— i.e., baby boomers—want to delay or ease into retirement. For many American adults of the postwar generation, the idea of retirement was nothing less than a dream come true. One day, usually at age 65, people would quit their jobs and begin a life of leisure, knowing that Social Security and whatever savings they had managed to accumulate over the years would be enough to live on. With life expectancy in the United States 67-years-old for men and 74-years-old for women in 1965, after all, one didn't need too much money to get through, on average, the next couple of years or decade. As well, Medicare, the national social insurance program, began that same year, with the federal government now picking up the medical and hospital bills for Americans 65 or older. Backed by the government entitlements of Social Security and Medicare, most older Americans could at least eke by and enjoy their golden years bouncing grandchildren on their knee, going out for early dinner at a local restaurant, and perhaps even spending the winter in a warm place like Florida or Arizona.[9]

A half-century-and-change later, this scenario is about as dated as the brand-new-at-the-time inventions of touch-tone phones and cassette tapes. Today, for a variety of economic and social reasons, "unretirement" is a far more viable model of living for older Americans than retirement, making it Plan A for baby boomers as they plunge headlong into their 60s and 70s. Even before Chris Farrell popularized the term with his 2014 book of that name, unretirement was offering many boomers an attractive option to the standard one-day-working-and-the-next-day-not-working model that was the rule for those around age 65. Farrell pushed the idea further, however, positing that it was in boomers' best interests to develop skills that would help them generate money well past the traditional retirement age. Working well into one's 60s or longer, even on a part-time basis, would make a major difference versus depending only on savings, should one have any.[10]

Waiting as long as possible to crack into one's nest egg was a smart investment strategy, Farrell continued, urging boomers to start thinking about their financial future as soon as possible. An income stream would also allow those in their early 60s to put off claiming Social Security benefits until they were 66 or 70, another wise financial move. Older adults who were not independently wealthy had better consider how to redefine themselves professionally, he argued, with the notion of unretirement far more sustainable than retirement. The trick, of course, is figuring out what to do should one's company force an older worker into retirement. For this group, how to translate one's skills into something new is key, unless one would be content making minimum wage and possibly tips in the hospitality industry.[11]

The emergence of unretirement is a function of the fact that not just most boomers but most Americans want to keep working as long as possible for both financial and emotional reasons. More than half of American workers plan to work past aged 65, according to a 2018 survey by the Transamerica Center for Retirement Studies, raising the implications of developing an age-friendly workplace.[12] Ensuring the presence of an inclusive, multigenerational workforce makes sense if only to avoid the economic and health-care train wreck and generational war that many are predicting for the country due to the tens of millions of boomers demanding their government entitlements. There is no doubt that a significant portion of boomers have not saved enough to live out their later years in comfort, more reason to make it possible for them to work as long as possible.[13]

Unretirement thus offers the big plus of turning baby boomers from an economic liability into a valuable asset. Well-educated, relatively healthy, and eager to work, boomers are, from a human resources perspective, ideal potential employees, with only ageism standing in the way of giving them the jobs they want, deserve, and are perfectly capable of doing. Sixty- and 70-somethings may not have been able to do the kind of factory and agricultural work that was common before Social Security was passed in 1935, but many, if not most, jobs today involve looking at a computer screen. As well, because interaction with other people is key to living longer, healthier lives, a robust job market for boomers would save the country billions in health-care costs, additional rationale to hope that unretirement gains traction in the years ahead.[14]

An age-friendlier workplace is especially important given that many older adults are continuing to work after they become eligible for full Social Security benefits at age 66. In a 2019 survey by Provision Living, respondents said they intended to stop working at an average of 72. Finances was mentioned most often (62%) as the reason to keep working, not surprisingly, with many saying they just couldn't afford to retire at an earlier age. But there were other reasons to stay at one's job, even if it was becoming more difficult to keep up and despite being the target of ageism. Forty-five percent still enjoyed working, 18% worked to avoid boredom, and 6% valued workplace camaraderie and said they would feel too lonely if they stopped working, according to the survey, interesting findings that bolster the argument that employees shouldn't be discarded simply because of their advanced age.[15]

Although just about 20% of Americans 65 years old or older were still working in 2018, that percentage was the highest it has been in more than half a century. Those with a college degree were more likely to remain in the workforce, as it was not unusual for less-educated workers to have to retire because of poor health or their job required a level of physical ability they no longer possessed. Experts call this spread (of about three years) "the retirement gap," a logical extension of the decades-long income disparity that exists between college and high school graduates. The former group has about three times the average retirement savings of the latter, a big difference that has major social and economic implications. Financial advisors typically tell their (nonwealthy) clients to keep working as long as possible so that they don't run out of money in their older age. Working until age 67 instead of 62 makes a huge difference in terms of retirement savings, another reason why an age-friendly workplace makes so much sense.[16]

Encore Careers

With unretirement becoming the norm, many baby boomers are embarking on second or "encore careers" after their original one, marking a major and perhaps even historic transformation of the workplace. After putting in 30 or 35 years at a job, some are deciding to call it quits or told to not bother coming in the following morning. City, state, and federal employees, like military personnel, public school teachers, police, firefighters, and garbage collectors, often have earned full retirement benefits by age 60, but many are not waiting at their mailboxes for their pension checks. Retirees of the "Greatest Generation" may have been happy to celebrate their final day on the job and sail off into the sunset, but most baby boomers have little interest in ending the productive phase of their lives. That most Americans plan to work past age 65 means that encore careers will play an ever-increasing role in the coming decades.[17]

Encore careers can also mean staying at the company at which one already works but in a different role. While widespread ageism in the workplace is a malevolent issue that needs to be addressed, a study by Cornell University found that many companies are starting to recognize the value of their aging workforce and are implementing flexible work arrangements to retain talent. Abbot, Lancaster Labs, and Hewlett Packard have provided work hour flexibility (reduced hours, job sharing, phased retirement, or part-year employment), for example, while Volkswagen of America and Mercy Health Systems have offered work schedule flexibility (flex schedule, annualized hours, or compressed work week). Dow Chemical Company, Duke Power, and CNA Insurance are companies that have allowed career flexibility (on/off ramps that include leaves, reduced responsibilities, job change/occupation shift, and phased retirements), while Quest Diagnostics, IBM, the U.S. Federal Government, Home Depot, Carondelet Health Network, and CVS/Caremark Pharmacies have made available flexibility of place (remote work, work from more than a single location, or "snow birding"). Finally, companies such as Hoffman-LaRoche, Principal Financial Group, SC Johnson, Busch Entertainment, the Aerospace Corporation, MIT, and Polaroid have built flexibility into the employment relationship itself (project work, consultant, temporary work), and Lincoln Financial Services, Baptist Health Systems, First Horizon National, and Mitretek have extended benefit flexibility (cafeteria plan, benefits during retirement, etc.). Organizations such as these have demonstrated a good understanding of older employees' long-term career plans, hopefully heralding the emergence of a more age-friendly workplace.[18]

By offering education and training to older adults to help them repurpose themselves, Encore.org is expanding the encore career marketplace while also serving social ends. Founded in 1997 by Marc Freedman as Civic Ventures, Encore.org has done much to advance the concept of encore careers while surfing the age wave of boomers. With their idealist roots, it's not surprising that millions of boomers are finding fulfillment in socially meaningful work. As I showed in my book *Boomers 3.0*, many boomers are actively engaged in the effort to "pay it forward," i.e., to give back to society in thanks for the rewards they earned during their first careers. Encore.org works with colleges and universities to develop programs that will enable older adults to find positions for the "greater good," a noble pursuit by any measure. Getting paid for work that blends one's personal passion with a social purpose (often in health care, education, or government) is an extremely powerful proposition that Encore.org is making real.[19]

AARP, too, is providing resources for older adults to fashion encore careers either at a nonprofit or through a Fortune 500 "transition program." AARP. org's Second Career section offers advice, online job search sites, and interesting mini-case histories of boomers who successfully made the jump from a traditional job into an encore career. At 61, for example, systems engineer Keith Gordon became a high school math teacher through IBM's "Transition to Teaching" program, while at age 57 Beverly Robinson transformed herself from a college provost to a goat farmer via a government technical assistance program. Sixty-seven-year-old Kate Young, meanwhile, redefined herself from the director of a nonprofit to a sustainable agricultural specialist through a Peace Corps program, and 59-year-old Noel Durrant from a quality and reliability program manager to a technology educator via an Intel Encore Fellowship. Such sanguine stories provide real-world evidence that encore careers for older adults are entirely possible and serve as a great example of age-friendly work.[20]

The Value of Experience

Just as AARP is leading the age-friendly community movement, so has the non-profit assumed a championing role in the creation of an age-friendly workplace. In 2018, the organization published a report titled "The Value of Experience: Age Discrimination Against Older Workers Persists," which was based on the findings from an extensive survey completed the previous year. The year 2017 was the 50th anniversary of the (feeble) ADEA of 1967, a good time to evaluate the effectiveness of the law. Workers aged 45 and older were polled on their experience in the workplace, especially with regard to the issue of discrimination. AARP knew that age-based bias was a fact of life, of course, but the survey would indicate the degree to which and the ways in which it was expressed.[21]

The findings were not pretty. Age discrimination in the American workplace was common, with three out of five older workers having seen it or experiencing it themselves. Very few workers (just 3%) filed a formal complaint to supervisors, HR, or a government agency, however, for reasons of which we can speculate. Most believed that age discrimination started when workers were in their 50s, with ageist comments from bosses or coworkers often the first indicator. Age discrimination often began even before an employee was hired; job applicants were commonly asked age-based questions in the interview process. While asking for birth or graduation date is not illegal, the answers can and are used to discriminate against older workers (which is illegal). Not surprisingly, then, older workers were reluctant to try to find a new job, knowing that having to disclose the year they were born or got out of college would likely squash the chances of receiving an offer.[22]

Interestingly, those polled were firm in their belief that legal protection against age discrimination wasn't strong enough, particularly when compared with the laws that served other groups. The Supreme Court did not have its best day in 1967; although the Court passed the ADEA, the Act made it difficult to prove age discrimination in the workplace. More than 90% of those surveyed felt that the nation's age discrimination laws should be strengthened, ideally to the level of the laws concerning race and gender. Lead researcher Rebecca Perron agreed. "With rich work histories, varied experiences and expertise, and work tenures that speak to commitment and resilience, older workers should have the opportunity to be judged on their merits rather than their age," Perron concluded, thinking that the findings of the study made it clear that major changes should be made if anything close to fairness and equity on the job was to be realized.[23]

Living, Learning, and Earning Longer

Some organizations would call it quits after conducting such research and reporting the findings but not AARP. In 2019, the nonprofit formed a partnership with the Geneva-based World Economic Forum (WEF) and the Paris-based Organisation for Economic Co-operation and Development (OECD) in what is called the "Living, Learning & Earning Longer" (LL&EL) learning collaborative. The aim of the global effort is to identify and share multigenerational, inclusive workforce practices in the hope that they will become the norm within all kinds of organizations, especially large corporations. Key to the effort is partnering with organizations that agree to the principles of the initiative; the growing list includes Bank of America, Fidelity Investments, Forbes Media, General Mills, and McKinsey & Company. Knowledge partners such as the Milken Institute, MIT AgeLab, and the Stanford Center on Longevity have also signed on to share research with the collaborative.[24]

The OECD's report "Promoting an Age-Inclusive Workforce" (subtitled "Living, Learning & Earning Longer") was proudly distributed when it was published in late 2020. The report "presents evidence on promising approaches, practical examples and ideas for successful multigenerational workplaces and provides a checklist on what employers can do to support and sustain age-friendly workplaces," the OECD stated, with a complementary digital learning platform also made available. The report concluded that employers need to act on three fronts in order to take advantage of the benefits to be gained by having an age-inclusive workforce: (1) attracting and retaining talent at all ages, (2) ensuring a good working environment and a healthy working life, and (3) developing and maintaining skills throughout careers.[25]

Like WHO's Global Network for Age-friendly Cities and Communities, the LL&EL initiative came about because of the long-term implications of an aging population. People are living longer and healthier lives, making the desire and need to keep working a fact of life. Increased longevity, combined with the demographic tidal wave of aging baby boomers, has changed the rules regarding how long people are expected to remain in the workforce. While governments can facilitate the process, it's really up to employers themselves to embrace the idea and practice of age-friendly work, as they do the hiring (and firing). Most important, perhaps, the research-based LL&EL makes it clear that a multigeneration workforce is good for all; not just employees but also employers (and governments) benefit from inclusivity. The actions to be taken are threefold: (1) ensuring that individuals remain employable throughout their lives, making continued education and training essential; (2) adopting and enforcing age-inclusive policies to prevent discrimination; and (3) providing opportunities for workers to not just keep working but also grow in their positions.[26]

All kinds of issues are embedded into the concept of living and working longer, making the initiative an ambitious but worthy pursuit. As a learning collaborative, the LL&EL has many questions that should be answered if its objectives are to be achieved. For example, what kind of organizational culture best facilitates inclusivity? Values such as respect, equity, security, and predictability come to mind, as does the notion that whatever kind of work is involved, it is meaningful in some way. Which standards and practices should be put in place in recruiting, assessing, retaining, and rewarding employees? Not just how to hire and evaluate workers goes into this equation but also where they can work and whether they can gradually phase out of their jobs. How can both employees and employers grow and prosper? Even if each is making money, neither should remain static if they are to realize their respective full potential.[27]

Most people think of technology first when it comes to the changing landscape of work, but the workforce itself is in major transition, the LL&EL initiative posits. With increased longevity, there may be five generations of people in a given workplace, something that should make human resources and "human capital" departments in organizations rethink their approach to staffing. Studies have shown that a diverse workforce performs better than one that isn't, correlating inclusivity with profitability. Embedded within the idea of a multigenerational workforce is, again, the possibility of flexibility. Rather than the standard Monday through Friday nine-to-five workday, more innovative companies around the world are allowing employees greater options in terms of when and where they work. A 60-year-old may very well want a different work schedule than a 30-year-old, for example, a good reason to build generational diversity into organizational culture.[28]

AARP and its partners, the WEF and OECD, wisely position a multigenerational workforce as a largely untapped resource that will lead to company growth. Just as racial and gender diversity are assets to any company, power resides in having employees of a wide range of ages, the organizations advise. Pairing the wisdom of a 70-year-old with the methodological skills of a recent business college grad can create interesting and synergistic sparks, and a worker with decades of experience has a trove of knowledge to pass on to a new 20-something hire. AARP backs up these nice stories with hard evidence. The stock prices of inclusive companies (not just in terms of age but also gender, race, sexuality, and ability) tend to outperform the S&P 500, a prime example of how employee diversity translates into financial gain. Rather than cost and decline, in other words, an age-friendly workplace represents upside economic potential that smart companies can and should take advantage of.[29]

Just as with combating ageism in general, myth-busting represents a big part of AARP's efforts to persuade more companies to have a multigenerational workforce. There's a "spillover effect" in productivity when employee teams are composed of mixed ages, a fact that counters the belief that output and efficiency decline when older people are on the job. When valuable things like knowledge transfer, mentoring, talent development, and reduced turnover are put into the mix, according to a 2020 study by Mercer, overall productivity has been shown to rise. Managers should look at the larger picture when it comes to evaluating the potential benefits of a multigenerational workforce, in other words, a more complicated task perhaps but a more accurate one.[30]

AARP also astutely makes a connection between the presence of older workers and attracting older consumers, something often overlooked by corporate types. "Companies whose employees reflect the diversity of a heterogeneous customer base establish stronger customer bonds and therefore stronger sales," AARP states, citing a McKinsey & Company study to support that claim. Older workers are likely to understand the wants and needs of older consumers not just because they of are a similar age but also because older workers are older consumers, a fact that frequently gets lost on human resources people eager to hire young people for marketing positions. Not only that, but older consumers spend more than younger ones (the former having accumulated more money and reached peak earning power), an additional reason to have a multigenerational workforce.[31]

AARP raises the stakes of workplace inclusivity by showing that age discrimination costs the United States hundreds of billions of dollars every year. The nation's economy missed out on an additional $850 billion in 2018, according to a 2020 OECD report, as countries with a higher percentage of workers over age 50 enjoyed increased gross domestic product (GDP). Should employment levels for such workers in America rise to the average level of other OECD member countries, the GDP per capita in the United States would increase about 8% by 2050. That may not sound like much, but it translates to a $3 trillion gain, hardly peanuts. Positioning an age-friendly American workplace as not just in employers' best interests but in the nation's as well is a marketing approach that many companies could learn from.[32]

AARP goes further by offering tools by which companies can determine their relative age friendliness, especially within the context of diversity and inclusion initiatives. Does your company include age within its initiative, assuming it has one? Does top management embrace the idea of a multigenerational workforce and take active steps to prevent age discrimination? Is hiring and the assignment of job responsibilities based on competencies rather than age? These and other questions are put to those who ask, with the answers feeding into an assessment score. Case studies and research are also offered, making AARP's website (aarpinternational.org) a go-to resource for organizations interested in bringing more age friendliness to their workplace.[33]

Knowledge Transfer

Although the anticipated mass exit of older adults from the workplace has yet to take place and perhaps never will, many executives remain concerned about the expertise that would disappear from their companies should it happen. After being at their jobs for decades, baby boomers would leave a vacuum of intellectual capital should they decide to quit *en masse*, the thinking goes, causing major problems that would take years from which to recover. Out of this concern has sprung the idea of "knowledge transfer"—the passing on of older workers' perspectives, insights, and skill sets to a generation of younger employees. Because it represents an asset—one of the few that older workers are considered to have, sadly—knowledge transfer can serve as a major enabler of age friendliness in the workplace.[34]

Handing over intellectual capital from one group of people to another is a complex process. Knowledge transfer incorporates not only the steps required to complete a certain task—how to run a meeting or how to write a document, say—but also how to think about and solve problems. Maintaining and building relationships with people on the outside is also part of the equation, as is how to best present the organization to the business community and general public. It ain't the first rodeo for employees in their 50s and 60s, one might say; those folks have been around long enough to have seen a similar issue or challenge many times before, something of great value in tackling a new one. In short, experience is a good thing for any organization, a fact that more high-level managers are realizing as they look at their older employees and wonder what to do if or when they decide to opt out.[35]

While the trend is to keep those paychecks rolling in as long as possible, some older workers are choosing to end their first careers, the impetus for companies to figure out how to best transfer those employees' knowledge to Gen Xers, millennials, and Gen Zers. "What's lost is a wealth of accumulated skills and experience, relationships and networks cultivated over years, and firsthand recollections about the development of products, services, and marketing strategies," wrote Eric F. Frazier for business.com. Employees in some organizations have experienced a scare when they realize that the only person who knows how to get a certain thing done, reach a specific contact, or locate a needed document has, like Elvis, left the building.[36]

Generational dynamics are playing a role in the transfer of workplace knowledge. While baby boomers and Gen Xers tend to communicate effectively, the former and millennials are believed to think and act differently, a perceived challenge for employers. (Millennials, defined as 18- to 34-year-olds, are the largest generation in the U.S. labor force, with one in three workers part of this 53.5 million-strong cohort. As millennials move through their 40s over the next decade, it should be noted, they too will begin to "age out" of many industries.) This idea of two-ships-passing-in-the-night between generations is clearly overstated, however, part of the divisive bucket-sorting that so-called experts in such things like to do. Many boomers have spent their careers as management analysts, industrial engineers, financial managers, labor relations managers, postal clerks, police detectives, registered nurses, social workers, and lawyers, according to the U.S. Bureau of Labor Statistics, making it those occupations in which there is likely to be a knowledge gap.[37]

As companies both large and small consider the idea of knowledge transfer, documenting how older employees do their jobs before they depart has become recognized as a means of avoiding a "brain drain." Much of this knowledge is experiential rather than written down, however, meaning it's not as simple as handing over a file folder. Losing technical knowledge is a particular concern for organizations whose senior engineers are planning to bow out. What is in workers' heads can't be simply replaced by a new hire, as literally no one is likely to have the "deep smarts" of a person who has held a particular job since the Reagan administration. Making the situation even more problematic is millennials' habit of changing jobs every few years, as they take their newly inherited knowledge with them when they walk out the door. (To be fair, boomers also job hopped like rabbits when they were in their 20s.)[38]

A variety of steps are being taken to allow older employees to pay their knowledge forward to younger ones. Some companies are creating diverse, intergenerational project teams, while others are putting boomers and millennials together in social settings outside the office to try to build workplace relationships. Job rotation exposes younger people to different parts of a business before they specialize in one particular area, and "job shadowing," where apprentices follow experienced workers around for a few months, has become another way to transfer knowledge. Many companies take videos of industry vets explaining a certain business process, a useful tool for more methodical tasks. General Motors has done as much as any company to retain institutional knowledge but at the same time has hired older ex-employees as consultants, a smart way to extend and spread their expertise. Baby boomers are directly responsible for one of the most successful business and production periods in American history, so companies should be doing whatever they can to enable the group to realize another great achievement: bestowing their knowledge for future generations.[39]

A New Social Contract

While knowledge transfer is an important card in older workers' deck should they want or need to play it, the simplest justification for an age-friendly workplace is that most of them want to stay put. Just 10% of Americans aged 65 and older were working in 1994, according to the Bureau of Labor Statistics, a dramatic shift in the nation's workplace dynamics over the course of a generation. Greater life expectancy has much to do with it, as most baby boomers plan on having another 20 years ahead of them if they did retire at age 65, like most of their "Greatest Generation" parents did. That's a long time for savings and investments to last, especially given boomers' more active (and expensive) lifestyles.[40] Ageism in the workplace is the impetus for some older workers to find alternative sources of income. Although it is the hoodie-clad 20-something who serves as the iconic image of the start-up founder, older Americans actually account for launching most new businesses in the country. Entrepreneurialism is in baby boomers' DNA, I think it's fair to say based on their history of innovation, and, if Big Business no longer wants them, they will create businesses of their own.

Elizabeth Isele has done much to pioneer entrepreneurship among older adults and advocate for an intergenerational workforce. Since 1998 (at age 56), Isele has led a movement to transform the concepts of aging and retirement by tapping into the experience of people ages 50 and older. Data from the Global Entrepreneurship Monitor and the Kaufman Foundation has shown that this group is starting businesses more than any other demographic and that 70% of their businesses are still operating five years out (compared to just 28% of young entrepreneurs' businesses).[41]

Isele's current gig is the Global Institute for Experienced Entrepreneurship (GIEE), an organization intended to leverage what she calls "the largest talent pool in history."

"Experience is a currency and a competitive advantage in today's economy, especially in the future of work and entrepreneurship," the GIEE states, the goal being to "unleash the power and potential of senior/experienced individuals to build economic prosperity for people of all ages worldwide." Through research, advocacy and public policy, and programs like Global Summits and an Experience Incubator®, the GIEE is doing much to advance what Isele calls "experieneurship."[42]

More attention is also being paid to age-friendly work because of its direct relationship to retirement, which remains an attractive option for some of those who can afford it. Findings from a 2020 global study of 15 countries revealed that workers will need 67% of their current annual salary in retirement, a figure that most employees simply won't realize if older employees continue to be forced out of their jobs. Extending employees' working lives is the most significant way that companies can enable retirees to have enough money to live on, but there are additional means, such as lengthening health-care benefits and offering flexible work arrangements. There's more to a job than a paycheck, the authors of the study (which included the Transamerica Center for Retirement Studies) concluded, and they call for a "new social contract" between employers and employees to avoid major financial problems in retirees' post-work lives.[43]

Phased retirement represents the potential of becoming a major clause within a new age-friendly social contract between employers and employees. Employees gradually transitioning out of their jobs is good for employers in that it cuts payroll costs, especially given the fact that older workers are likely to be higher paid than younger ones. Also, an older worker staying partly on the job allows for knowledge transfer and mentoring. For the employee, phased retirement allows him or her to pad their nest egg and ease the emotional issues that often come with not working. Because jobs provide significant purpose and meaning in one's life and serve as an important component of personal identity, a sudden end to working can prove to be a traumatic experience. Although there are many uncertainties that need to be resolved—mostly the question of employees continuing to receive benefits—phased retirement could be the best option in achieving an age-friendly workplace.[44]

Phased retirement, job flexibility, and other such steps are all welcome developments, of course, but they are mere fix-its to a much bigger problem. While age-friendly communities are taking the country by storm, the prospect of age-friendly work has been more of a trickle. It is true that a few dozen top execs of major corporations have signed up for AARP's LL&EL initiative, knowing that doing so helps their public profile (and perhaps because those folks are likely to themselves to be older employees!). Neither the philosophy nor the practice has yet to work its way down through the ranks, however, as lingering stereotypes and an attitude of business as usual are difficult to change. Until companies realize that age inclusivity really does improve the bottom line, just as AARP convincingly shows, older workers will continue to be discriminated against.

There are, however, signs that some progress is being made. Forbes Media— not a company that one might think would be a strong advocate for an age-friendly workplace given its deep ties to Corporate America—is a loud voice of literally business-as-usual discrimination. A few of the titles of articles the print and online magazine published in 2020—"Ageism is Forcing Older Workers Out of the Job Market," "Gendered Ageism is the New Sexism," "Ageism is Not Just a Disease—It's the New Business Model for Top Ad Agencies," and "Career

Coaches Advise on How to Fight Back Against Ageism"—indicate the coura-geous commitment the media company is making to address the issue. Forbes has also partnered with AARP's LL&EL initiative, more reason to believe that C-suite management is receptive to the idea of age friendliness. MediaVillage, which describes itself as "the media industry's education and diversity center of excellence," is also deeply committed to fighting ageism in the workplace. The website (to which I occasionally contribute) includes a column called "The Age of Aging," another example of Big Business at least acknowledging the problem.

Things are percolating at the local level as well. Just as Colorado was at the forefront of the age-friendly community movement, so is the state taking the lead in combating workplace ageism. Through the Changing the Narrative initiative, businesses in the state can earn the Certified Age-Friendly Employer (CAFE) classification, something not unlike the much-sought designations of "Best Places to Work" and "Healthiest Places to Work." Being named to those latter groups is important because they help companies attract the best talent, and the same is hoped for the CAFE classification. Boston-based Age Friendly Foundation is promoting CAFE by formally recognizing those employers that maintain policies, practices, and programs supporting people aged 50 or older. A confidential CAFE assessment is based on a dozen categories (recruitment, retention, training and development, health-care benefits, etc.) As of June 2020, AT&T, the Home Depot, Starbucks, and Walgreens were some of the compa-nies that had earned the CAFE certification.[45]

Also blazing the age-friendly trail of work in Colorado is the NextFifty Ini-tiative, a private foundation dedicated to funding mission-driven objectives that improve the lives of older adults and their caregivers. Improving and sustain-ing the quality of life for people in "their second 50 years," as the organization describes it, is the goal. The NextFifty Initiative also serves as an educational resource and advocates for transformational change. "We consider ourselves an engine for innovation that transforms aging," NextFifty states on its website, believing that their work will "impact life for generations to come." The needs of low- and moderate-income persons are prioritized as are individuals with physi-cal, cognitive, and/or behavioral disabilities.[46]

Unlock the Potential

Such initiatives are spot-on if we are to see a truly age-friendly workplace emerge in the foreseeable future, but much more needs to be done. Companies have staffed up with D&I people, but discrimination based on race and gender remains their focus, with little if any attention paid to equally virulent age bias. Just as it often farms out specialized knowledge to outside experts, Big Business is also now bringing in consultants to help employees avoid discriminatory practices. A number of consulting groups have recently popped up to provide training and development in the area of diversity and inclusion, but again, ageism is not considered a priority. Top D&I consultants, according to Forbes.com, include Dr. Nika White, Deborah Levine, Steven Matley, Wayne Sutton, Mary-Frances Winters, and Anj Handa.[47]

One consultancy dedicated to ending age discrimination at work is the San Antonio-based Age Equity Alliance (AEA). AEA is a 501(c)(3) focused on increasing age equity in the workplace through education and training, showing organizations how to "unlock the potential" of their people. Age equity in the workplace refers to "building a base of talent *across the age spectrum* to maximize cognitive diversity, increase innovation and decision-making, and improve business outcomes," AEA states, citing studies showing that outcomes are improved when all forms of diversity are embraced. Age equity is important if only because of the numbers; those 65 years old and older represent the fastest-growing age group, making them a valuable pool of talent for all kinds of jobs.[48]

By emphasizing that achieving age equity in the workplace is a matter of education, AEA offers a sensible approach to the often complicated and challenging arena of diversity and inclusion. "We believe education creates an awareness that leads to action and change," AEA explains, with research and executive coaching just a couple of tools used to facilitate the process. Course offerings include "How to Build an Age Inclusive Workplace," "Social Innovation and Age Equity: Why Business & Society Need Both," "Age Equity in Recruitment, Development, and Retention," "Intersectionality: How to Reduce the Double and Triple Threat of Bias (Gender + Sexuality + Race + Age)," "How a Culture of Belonging Increases Innovation and Productivity," "The Power of (Age) Diversity to Drive Innovation," "Steps for Embedding Age Equity in Diversity, Equity, and Inclusion Strategy," and "The Complexity of Age and Aging in the Workplace (Implicit and Unconscious Bias)."[49]

Before working with a client, AEA often conducts what it calls an "age equity evaluation" to determine strengths, weaknesses, opportunities, and threats to age inclusivity. How does the organization compare to others within its industry in terms of age representation and other relevant criteria? The answer to that question lays the foundation for how to best progress workplace age equity. Companies usually do a good job in presenting gender, race, and ethnic diversity in images on their websites, for example, but frequently forget about age. Take a look at some corporate websites and you'll see groups of happy young people of a wide variety of skin shades but few if any employees or clients who were born before 1970. Such external content suggests that the organization is not complying with the ADEA and, even worse, reinforces the belief that older people simply don't warrant being part of a workforce.[50]

Beyond its educational and training services, the AEA has adeptly used You-Tube to get its much-needed message across. Sheila Callaham, chair of AEA (and a contributor to Forbes.com), has lots to say on the subject of age equity in the workplace, and she regularly posts research-based videos that reflect her insightful views. These content-rich, bite-sized informational nuggets are fonts of wisdom from which managers can learn much. Don't subscribe to generational generalities, Callaham advised in one post, such as, for example, the tired trope that Gen Zers prefer to communicate by texts while baby boomers like to make phone calls. Another myth is that employees of different generations don't like working together, a claim as wrongheaded as men and women or blacks and whites not wanting to be on the same team. Such stereotyping widens the age divide, precisely opposite of what we should do to advance age equity at and outside of work. Perhaps the most important point Callaham makes is that by tolerating age discrimination in the workplace and in society as a whole, we are passing on our biases to younger generations.[51] We have the opportunity and responsibility to break this pattern by making a commitment to making the workplace a lot more age friendly.

Notes

1 Jim Miller, "Tips and Resources for Older Job Seekers," *Honolulu Star-Advertiser*, March 20, 2018.
2 "Tips and Resources for Older Job Seekers."
3 Patricia G. Barnes, *Overcoming Age Discrimination in Employment: An Essential Guide for Workers, Advocates & Employers* (Tucson: Patricia G. Barnes, 2016) 1–2.
4 Patricia G. Barnes, *Betrayed: The Legalization of Age Discrimination in the Workplace* (Tucson: Patricia G. Barnes, 2014).
5 Patti Temple Rocks, *I'm Not Done: It's Time to Talk About Ageism in the Workplace* (Lioncrest Publishing: Austin, TX, 2019) 13–17.
6 Lisa Taylor and Fern Lebo, *The Talent Revolution: Longevity and the Future of Work* (Toronto, CA: Rotman-UTP Publishing, 2019) vii–viii.
7 Chip Conley, *Wisdom at Work: The Making of a Modern Elder* (New York: Currency, 2018) 2–3.
8 Nellie Bowles, "A New Luxury Retreat Caters to Elderly Workers in Tech (Age 30 and Up)," *New York Times (Online)*, March 4, 2019.
9 Lawrence R. Samuel, *Boomers 3.0: Marketing to Baby Boomers in Their Third Act of Life* (Santa Barbara, CA: Praeger, 2017) 34–35.
10 *Boomers 3.0* 35.
11 *Boomers 3.0* 35.
12 Paul Davidson, "Millennials, Gen Xers to Baby Boomers: Can You Retire So I Can Get a Job Promotion?" *USA Today*, November 7, 2019.

13 *Boomers 3.0* 36.

14 *Boomers 3.0* 36.

15 Michael S. Fischer, "Why Seniors Are Delaying Retirement," *ThinkAdvisor*, October 4, 2019.

16 Stan Choe and Sarah Skidmore Sell, "Working Past 65? It's Easier, to a Degree," *Telegraph-Herald (Dubuque, Iowa)*, October 14, 2018, D3.

17 *Boomers 3.0* 37.

18 *Boomers 3.0* 37–38.

19 *Boomers 3.0* 38.

20 *Boomers 3.0* 38.

21 "The Value of Experience: Age Discrimination Against Older Workers Persists," *AARP Research*, 2018.

22 "The Value of Experience: Age Discrimination Against Older Workers Persists."

23 "The Value of Experience: Age Discrimination Against Older Workers Persists."

24 "Living, Learning & Earning Longer," aarpinternational.org.

25 "Promoting an Age-Inclusive Workforce: Living, Learning and Earning Longer," Paris: OECD, 2020.

26 aarpinternational.org.

27 aarpinternational.org.

28 aarpinternational.org.

29 aarpinternational.org.

30 aarpinternational.org.

31 aarpinternational.org.

32 aarpinternational.org.

33 aarpinternational.org.

34 *Boomers 3.0* 137.

35 *Boomers 3.0* 137.

36 *Boomers 3.0* 137–138.

37 *Boomers 3.0* 138.

38 *Boomers 3.0* 138.

39 *Boomers 3.0* 138–139.

40 Candace Moody, "Boomers Look to Keep Working On," *Florida Times Union*, October 19, 2016, D1.

41 Julia Randell-Khan, "An Interview with Elizabeth Isele: Tapping into Elders Entrepreneurial Mindset Boosts Economic Prosperity for All Ages," *Aging Today*, September/October 2019, 10.

42 experieneurship.com.

43 "Age-Friendly Employers are Integral to the New Social Contract for Retirement," *PR Newswire*, June 24, 2020.

44 Barry Kozak, "Phased Retirement Programs as part of an Age-Friendly Business Strategy," *Benefits Law Journal*, Winter 2018, 57.

45 "CAFE Certification Combats Workplace Ageism," *TD: Talent Development*, June 2020.

46 next50initiative.org.

47 forbes.com.

48 ageequityalliance.org.

49 ageequityalliance.org.

50 ageequityalliance.org.

51 ageequityalliance.org.

Chapter 4

Age-Friendly Marketing

A vibrant longevity economy is already developing as markets recognize the demand for products and services to meet the needs of the massive aging demographic.

Paul Irving
Chair of the Milken Institute
Center for the Future of Aging, 2020

In March 2019, a few dozen white-haired folks boarded a bus at Laguna Woods Village, a retirement community in Southern California. Where were these mostly 70- and 80-somethings, some using canes and pushing walkers, going? One might say to the happiest place on Earth, but it wasn't Disneyland, which was just a few miles away. Rather, the group was off to the Bud and Bloom marijuana dispensary in Santa Ana, where they would spend the next few hours eating a light lunch, playing a few games of bingo, and selecting their next month's supply of cannabis-infused products. "It's like the ultimate senior experience," said one of the retirees; he, like the others, was interested in the therapeutic value of cannabis rather than its mind-altering properties. Baby boomers and even some of the Greatest Generation represent the fastest-growing segment of the CBD industry, finding medical marijuana to be of considerable help in chronic pain management, anxiety, and sleeplessness. Some users had been taking dozens of prescribed pills a day, many of them opiates, for their conditions but swapped those out for an herbal gummy or chocolate bar and were pleased with the results.[1]

Bingo and pot were a nice mix of ingredients in the creation of what I call age-friendly marketing—efforts by the business community that resonate with older consumers. Just as Big Business underserves people in their 50s and older

DOI: 10.4324/9781003196235-5

by discriminating against them as workers, so does it treat them unfairly as consumers. This shouldn't come as too surprising, as ageism serves as a powerful common denominator in both the earning and spending of money. There is, in other words, a direct relationship between Corporate America's adamant refusal to hire and retain older employees and its overt snubbing of older consumers. This is not only strange, given the sound reasons not to do either, but also profoundly disturbing. For better or worse, our society runs on consumer capitalism, making the exclusion of citizens in their third act of life on both ends of the process one of our nation's worst features.

Fortunately, as the various tentacles of the age-friendly movement spread throughout society, more marketers are beginning to appreciate the opportunities being missed. Even if it is more about increasing the bottom line than doing the right thing, smarter managers at smarter organizations are recognizing that older consumers—specifically baby boomers—represent too big and wealthy a market to ignore. Age-friendly marketing is a means by which we can lessen ageism in America, a good thing for society as a whole.

Old Age Is Made Up

In his *The Old Rush: Marketing for Gold in the Age of Aging*, Peter Hubbell pinpointed 2014 as a turning point in marketing, as it was then that the youngest baby boomer would become 50 years old. As the CEO of BoomAgers, a marketing and communications consultancy dedicated to the baby boomer market, Hubbell was naturally happy to report the news that older consumers were a huge target audience that should not go ignored (18- to 49-year-olds had long been marketers' sweet spot). Hubbell went so far as to trademark baby boomers as the Most Valuable Generation™, their numbers and wealth just too sizable for businesses to resist despite all the stereotypes that have long been attached to older consumers. Trillions of dollars were at stake and, best of all, aging was a global phenomenon, the basis for the titular "old rush," which Hubbell described as "the next chance to strike it rich in marketing."[2]

Seeing gold in them thar hills, Hubbell followed up his *The Old Rush* with his 2015 *Getting Better with Age: Improving Marketing in the Age of Aging*. Although he switched metaphors—moving from mining for precious metal to wine and other things that improve with age—Hubbell stayed true to the message that baby boomers were a vital but still largely ignored segment of the marketplace. It was marketers who needed to change their ways, he argued, as the kind of standard thinking and usual approaches used to communicate with older consumers hearkened back to a different era.[3]

I took a more cultural perspective in my own *Boomers 3.0: Marketing to Baby Boomers in Their Third Act of Life* of 2017, arguing that most business books were, well, too businessy. My goal was to contextualize business objectives within a culturally based, forward-thinking framework in order to leverage what I felt was the biggest story of our time and place—our aging population. My main point was to show that the often-distressing changes to one's body in one's third act of life (hence *Boomers 3.0*) are often countered by an evolution of mind and spirit, with those years typically a period of intellectual growth, accelerated creativity, emotional contentedness, and a desire to take on new challenges. Because boomers were reinventing the concept of older age, however, I questioned whether organizations should even think in terms of a market segment made up of "old" people—a question that I continue to ponder.[4]

Decent fodder, if I may say so, but it was Joseph F. Coughlin's *The Longevity Economy: Unlocking the World's Fastest-Growing, Most Misunderstood Market* that quickly became the seminal resource of age-friendly marketing. Coughlin, the head of MIT's AgeLab (a research organization devoted to studying the intersection of aging and business), was in a unique position to map out the larger consequences of human longevity. While other megatrends like climate change, geopolitics, and technological advancements were no doubt game changers, the certainty of global aging made it the most profound of shifts to come. Coughlin's primary (and rather startling) argument was that, in his words, "old age is made up," meaning the concept of "oldness" was a social construct. While my knees might disagree with that claim, it can be seen how segmenting the population in certain ways, especially by age, has served certain economic, social, and political ends. As others have suggested, the narrative of aging is much different than the reality, triggering a bevy of problems that do real damage to peoples' lives.[5]

Coughlin and his fellow AgeLabers believe that many of those problems can be solved by bridging the worlds of aging and business in ways that have yet to be done. If successful, the results will be far more impactful than an easier-to-use can opener or larger-print product labeling. "By building a vision of late life that is more than just a miserable version of middle age, companies won't just be minting money, helping older people and their caregivers, and making aging societies more viable," Coughlin wrote, but "also be creating a cultural environment that values the contributions of older adults." Age-friendly marketing thus has the potential of taking much of the wind out of the sails of ageism, thereby leveling the playing field of the workplace and in community life.[6]

Academics tuned into the real-world dynamics of age-friendly marketing have also weighed in with keen insights. In their article "Aging as an Engine of Innovation, Business Development, and Employment Growth" published in the *Economic Development Journal* in 2018, James H. Johnson Jr., Allan

M. Parnell, and Huan Lian provided a scholarly take on how aging should be treated as an opportunity versus a challenge. While challenges do indeed exist—primarily those relating to social safety nets for what the authors call the "frail elderly"—the University of North Carolina at Chapel Hill professors saw the aging of America as something that can offer organizations many potential rewards. Whether it was advancing the lives of the "active old" or caring for the "nonactive old," the prospect of many more people in their third act of life in this country was a good thing, if only more businesspeople could see it that way. "Aspiring entrepreneurs and existing business enterprises that recognize the propitious opportunity to drive innovation by creating products and services that promote successful aging and create age-friendly communities can potentially shape U.S. economic and employment growth in the foreseeable future," they wrote, a solid if a bit egg-heady endorsement of age-friendly marketing.[7]

Johnson, Parnell, and Lian went further by outlining four BIG (their emphasis) opportunities related to aging in America. Big Opportunity #1 is "The Innovation Challenge," which correctly argues that venture capitalists have focused too much on designing products to help wealthier older people age in place and not enough on services that can help the broader population lead more independent lives. Big Opportunity #2, "Boomer Purchasing Power," suggests that marketers have overemphasized physical and cognitive problems like arthritis, incontinence, and dementia, not realizing that many of those 65 or older are still working and living much like they did decades earlier. Big Opportunity #3, "Demand for Senior Care Workers," shows that more than a million more senior care workers will be needed in just a few years and many more than that over the next couple of decades. Finally, Big Opportunity #4, "Fixing Spaces and Places," is about the need to make buildings, whether residential, commercial, or public, more age friendly, more so than what is currently required to comply with the Americans with Disabilities Act (a 1990 civil rights law that mandates accessibility standards for those with restricted mobility, hearing, and vision impairment to access places of public accommodations).[8]

Marketers seeking opportunities to be had by surfing the "age wave" should also listen to the man who coined that term. Since the late 1980s, Ken Dychtwald, the founder of the speaking and consulting firm Age Wave, has been perhaps the most respected authority on aging and what businesses should do about it. In his and Robert Morison's 2020 *What Retirees Want: A Holistic View of Life's Third Age*, the authors examined how baby boomers are changing (or rejecting) retirement and what that means for marketers. Rather than being an end to one's active life or the segue to gradual decline, retirement can be a beginning, Dychtwald and Morison argue, filled with freedom and purpose. Baby boomers "see retirement as an opportunity for new dreams, contributions, and personal reinventions with new interests, relationships, and ways of living," they write, offering "new experiences and new ways to learn."[9]

No One over 40

In their book, Dychtwald and Morison also took time to show how many marketers get it wrong in communicating with baby boomers, if they communicate with them at all. "Most marketers direct much of their attention to millennials and Gen Zers," they wrote, even though members of those generations are "predominantly cash-strapped, time-constrained, and only marginally loyal to products and services." The authors then cited a number of marketers who have aired ageist commercials, including E-Trade (octogenarian lifeguard and firefighter) and Tide (grandpa in underwear looking for pants). Poking fun at older adults is tolerated, considered humorous, while taking a similar approach with women, people of color, or the LGBTQ community is a whole different matter. Given the general feelings about older people and lack of knowledge in how to connect with them, it's easier to just leave them out of advertising, a good number of companies conclude. Indeed, while Americans over 50 account for 70% of consumer spending, they represent just 15% of the people in media and advertising, according to a 2019 study by AARP, a reflection of their relative cultural invisibility.[10]

A big part of the problem is who is creating the ads. The American (and British) advertising industry is notoriously youth-centric, a function of two different things. First is the (false) premise that youth is equated with creativity and innovation; people in their 20s and 30s are naturally imbued with the ability to think out of the box and come up with great campaigns, this idea goes, while the right sides of brains 40 years old or older are considered to have mostly shriveled up. Second is money; older employees usually cost more because they are more experienced, so ad agencies, under pressure to cut costs by their penny-pinching holding companies, are eager to replace them with younger, cheaper (and more creative!) talent.[11] "In advertising, ageism is a tricky challenge because it is bifurcated," Lauren Tucker, CEO and founder of the consultancy Do What Matters, told me, saying that "there are a lot of older boomers and members of the Silent Generation at the top that are seen by millennials as hoarding opportunity." Older people seeking middle management positions find it hard to get hired by millennials, a decision often endorsed by agency leaders (who ironically are in the same older generational cohort). Tucker, one of the best diversity, equity, and inclusion advisors in business today, uses what she calls "inclusion nudges" in all talent development and management practices, the goal being to "debias certain processes while elevating the differences that are relevant to client solutions."

Given the obsession with youth in the ad business, it should perhaps come as no surprise that the commercials it makes are decidedly age unfriendly. AARP's study revealed that when they were depicted in the media, older people were rarely shown at work, as younger people often were. (This despite the fact that more than 53 million people older than 50 are employed, making up a third of the American labor force, according to the Bureau of Labor Statistics.) It was not unusual for older people to be seen in the company of a medical professional but almost never handling technology, reinforcing the false image of them as unhealthy Luddites. "The demographic is shunned and caricatured in marketing images, perpetuating unrealistic stereotypes and contributing to age discrimination," wrote Tiffany Hsu of the *New York Times* in reporting AARP's findings.[12]

Through its #DisruptAging campaign, AARP is making some headway in changing perceptions about representations of age in both advertising and the workplace. "Disrupt Aging is a place to have a new conversation about how we want to live and age," the much-needed campaign states, its mission to "celebrate all those who own their age." Exposing ageism is part of the goal, with advertising used to illustrate the very real biases held against older consumers and workers.[13] In the first ad it produced for the campaign, AARP put a hidden camera on a food truck with a sign in front saying that only people under 40 would be served. Each customer that approached the beignet truck was asked by the order taker if he or she fit the demographic and if not was turned away. "You're just not what we're looking for," one 40+ person was told, another that "older people just don't fit into our culture." Some noncustomers were understandably angry, just the kind of response needed to spark action and create change.[14]

Ageist marketing is all the more absurd when what is alternatively called "the silver surge," "the silver economy," or "the gray dollar" arguably represents the biggest opportunity in business for the next couple of decades. Much has been written about the value of connecting with older consumers, but marketers themselves have been reluctant to do so because of ageist thinking. "Companies tend to neglect older generations, focusing instead on millennials and Gen Z," wrote Andrea Felsted for bloomberg.com in 2021, thinking that in the future, "such a strategy will be costly." Beyond all the myths and stereotypes surrounding older consumers, many marketers typically focus on household income versus net worth, mistakenly assuming that less money coming in means less money can go out. While there are certain differences between older consumers and younger ones—the latter tend to spend less on fashion and beauty but more on food, travel, and technology, according to the Mature Marketing Association—way too much is made of the role of age in the marketplace.[15]

Just as it has shown the benefits to be had from age-friendly communities and an age-friendly workplace, AARP has demonstrated the value of the longevity economy to the business community and the nation as a whole. This time partnering with the Economist Intelligence Unit, AARP produced a report called "The Longevity Economy Outlook," which documents the rather staggering numbers that are in play. "Private sector leaders now have the chance to seize this economic opportunity and harness the power of the 50-plus cohort," the report stated, citing $8.3 trillion in annual economic activity in 2018. That number will get even larger in the coming decades as that age group swells to 41% of the country's total population in 2050, an opportunity too big to ignore. Put a different way, 56 cents of every dollar was spent by 50-plussers in the United States, a figure forecast to 61 cents by 2050. "U.S. businesses will gain from appraising what this ongoing demographic transformation means for their sales strategies, product development and services, and workforce," AARP advised, urging companies both big and small to invest in the older consumer market.[16]

As such numbers make clear, the longevity economy is built around the fact that baby boomers collectively have a ton of money. (Need it be said, a sizable number of the group have little or no resources at all and are or will be dependent on Social Security and Medicare just to get by.) Much has been made about "the wealth gap" between generations, and with good reason. In 2016, Americans 50 years old and older held 84% of all investable assets, up from 69% in 1989, according to the Fed's triennial Survey of Consumer Finances. Wealth disparity is even more polarized when comparing the oldest and youngest adults. In 1989, the median household aged 65 to 75 held almost eight times more wealth than families headed by 25- to 35-year-olds. By 2016, according to the St. Louis Fed, the median baby boomer had nearly 13 times more wealth than the average millennial. From this perspective, marketers' orientation toward millennials and Gen Z (who are even poorer) makes little if no sense, as boomers simply have more purchasing power.[17]

Boomers' transfer of wealth to their children has also made headlines, but most of them are not quite ready to open their wallets. In fact, it is boomers who are inheriting money, and a lot of it. Boomers inherited about $9 trillion between 1989 and 2016, a 2019 study by the retirement planning firm United Income found, with much of this money going toward medical bills and savings. Whatever remains of boomers' wealth will indeed be passed on to heirs and given to charities—a whopping $36 trillion, it is estimated—but this will take about 30 years to happen. Until they have no more need for money—you can't take it with you, as they say—boomers will actively find ways to spend it.[18]

Much of this wealth will belong to women. By 2030, American women are expected to control $30 trillion in financial assets, according to McKinsey & Company, about three times the current number. The jump is mostly due to the fact that life expectancy for women is greater than that for men; wives will inherit the wealth from their husbands. As well, younger women are becoming more financially astute, this too accounting for the gender-based shift. This huge transfer of wealth poses major implications for marketers in all kinds of product and service categories but none more than the financial industry. Traditionally male-dominated industries such as automotive and real estate have done a decent job in recent years appealing to female consumers, something wealth management firms can and should aspire to do.[19]

Aging Is an Opportunity

One organization taking an encouraging thought leadership role in age friendly marketing is the Global Coalition on Aging (GCOA). "Aging is an opportunity," declares the New York–based organization, echoing AARP's grand thesis that longer longevity demands that both public policymakers and the private sector rethink their long-term plans. Many see disaster looming as the planet's population becomes older, but GCOA flips that viewpoint around by correctly pointing out that major social transformation presents significant upside potential. Change may be difficult, but institutions and organizations that can see where the future is headed are likely to benefit in a big way. "Silver is the new green," the GCOA advises, ready to help like-minded companies and individuals to seize the aging day.[20]

The GCOA claims to be the world's leading business voice on aging-related policy and strategy, an assertion it backs up by taking on some mighty big initiatives. Education is often the first step, as not just the general public but also many elected officials and businesspeople who are considered experts in a particular field have little idea about the size and scope of the approaching age wave. Forming partnerships is typically the next step, with the GCOA helping organizations and institutions tap into the opportunities to be had in terms of both the marketplace and workforce. The GCOA focuses on three areas: (1) the silver economy, i.e., how older people can drive growth and productivity as workers; (2) health and wellness, specifically new products and services that will help people not just live longer but better; and (3) elder care, the new models of caregiving that must be developed as demand for such services rises.[21]

While the GCOA is unapologetically wonky, the organization is sparking considerable dialogue and constructive change via its white papers, roundtables, webinars, and presentations. (Information about COVID-19 has, not surprisingly, taken priority since March 2020.) By putting people from a diverse array of backgrounds together in a room, whether real or virtual, perspectives and learnings are necessarily shared, precisely what needs to happen to realize positive outcomes. Members of the GCOA include companies from the health, pharmaceuticals, technology, and financial services industries, such as

AEGON, Bank of America, Bayer, Deloitte, Intel, Lilly, Pfizer, and Phillips. Non-governmental organizations and advocacy groups, academics, and governments have also signed up.[22]

Just looking at an actuarial table leads one to take the longevity economy very seriously. (Many of us who make it to older age have a good chance of living into our 90s, not to mention the fact that a child born in the developed world today has a very good chance of living to 100). Although the workplace has much to do with it, Susan Wilner Golden and Laura Carstensen of the Stanford Center on Longevity (SCOL) defined the longevity economy as the purchasing power of people 55 and over, a simple but compelling way of getting businesses to invest in it. There's nothing wrong with coming up with a new gadget targeted at older people, but baking the concept into business strategy offers much more potential. In its work with Bank of America, the SCOL developed a framework to help its financial advisors guide clients through the retirement (or unretirement) process. The company even hired a "financial gerontologist" to be part of the program, an interesting take on the often complicated relationship between money and aging. The initiative not only proved to be a valuable resource for Bank of America (and its wealth management firm Merrill Lynch) but also reportedly changed the company's culture, a great example of the value of age-friendly marketing.[23]

Paul Irving, chair of the Milken Institute Center for the Future of Aging, has done an excellent job counterbalancing the undeniable challenges associated with global aging with its opportunities. Irving has made the good point that the already staggering figures forecast for an older population may actually be low should advances in bioscience push average human longevity further, even by a few years. Irving also brings a macro perspective to the table by reminding us that our basic institutions—work, education, and health care, notably—are primarily designed to serve the needs of younger adults. The unprecedented demographic shift that is already in progress is somewhat analogous to climate change, he suggests, in that a failure to act would likely be very costly, both socially and economically. "Thankfully, an alternative future, one that adapts well to aging, holds the promise of strengthening societies, expanding economies and improving life for people of all ages," Irving wrote in the Institute's *Journal of Economic Policy* in 2020, happy to see that "age friendly housing, workplaces, and transit systems are evolving."[24]

More populist voices are making a solid case for marketers to get a piece of the silver economy, illustrating how broadly the age-friendly movement really is. Silver Disobedience, for example, comes at the opportunity in a much different way than think tanks, not surprising given that the company was founded by an ex-Wilhelmina model. In 2017, Dian Griesel started the website and consulting platform "with the belief that every age is relevant and that aging is the process whereby we get to know ourselves and others more deeply and with greater kindness over time." Griesel claims to have offered her insights on aging to many organizations and individuals (and has been regularly hired as a "silver" model to appeal to the "48 to 100+" demographic). While I'm not actually sure where the "disobedience" comes in, Griesel reportedly reels in millions of readers every month to her blog for news on silver health, travel, and living, part of the growing age-friendly community.[25]

As the chorus of voices, both high and low, proclaiming the business opportunities that are associated with aging gets louder, more venture capitalists are gradually gravitating to the area. Silicon Valley start-ups have historically been slow to invest in companies planning to offer products and services to older consumers, perhaps because these kinds of businesses lack the sexiness of a new gaming app or video-sharing website. But as more rich folks get older or have a personal experience with someone who is facing a physical or cognitive challenge that has come along with aging, dollars are beginning to pour into such start-ups. Primetime Partners is one venture capital fund taking a one-stop-shop approach by seeing opportunities in a wide variety of services, including caregiving, nutrition, entertainment, and technology. The kind of businesses Primetime Partners is prepared to invest in range from aging in place (e.g., senior living, social housing, home renovation, and Internet of things monitoring), financial security (e.g., aging-specific financial products and employment for older adults), care management, social determinants of health (e.g., fitness/fall prevention, social isolation), longevity health care (e.g., cognitive preservation and care and auditory/eyesight care), and consumer experiences (e.g., media and travel). Caregivers themselves are a large and growing market, suggesting that there will be more entrepreneurs keen on starting companies that offer products and services to that sizable group as well.[26]

Those with a vested interest in seeing more venture capital put into age-friendly businesses are not surprisingly dangling the juicy carrot of the forecasted $8.3 trillion longevity economy. Mary Furlong, a long-time authority in the aging space, has for the past few years organized events and conferences to bring together those working in the life sciences and venture capital people to accelerate the funding of related early stage companies. "The need for advancements in drugs, devices, diagnostics and digital health for the treatment of age-related conditions is crucial," Furlong said in 2021, partnering with a company called Life Science Nation to produce the What's Next Longevity Summit. "We are in a golden age of technology and the AgeTech arena needs a partnering event such as we are presenting to help connect the global capital," Furlong added; her summit was designed to matchmake experts from AARP and the NIA with health-care and tech execs, as well as VCs like Primetime Partners and Stanley Ventures (part of Stanley Black & Decker).[27]

A Bogus Image

Most of VC's "AgeTech" money is based on the assumption that aging baby boomers will age in place. While some boomers—especially those from the Northeast and Midwest, where the cost of living can be high and the temperature can be low—are planning to head south, many are indeed deciding to stay put in their communities and, if possible, homes. The desire to age in place has emerged as a defining trait of baby boomers as they move through their 60s and 70s. Being close to relatives is a big factor in this decision, as is the simple fact that most feel comfortable in the homes in which they have lived, often for decades. Starting over in a new town and a new house or condo understandably doesn't appeal to many, even if tempted by lower taxes or year-round golf.[28]

With millions of baby boomers intent on staying in their homes, sweet homes, there is much opportunity to make marketing directed to them more age friendly. It is true that many older people will need to make changes to their homes as they age in place in order to make living there easier and, especially, safer. Widened doorways (to accommodate wheelchairs, if necessary), additional lighting, grab handles, and nonslip floors are renovations that can make a big difference in the everyday lives of older people. Those who can afford it may be replacing stairs with ramps, putting in elevators (or escalators!), and redoing their kitchens and bathrooms to make them easier to use.[29]

While such renovations fill a need, there is a downside. "Products designed for older people reinforce a bogus image of them as passive and feeble," argued Joseph Coughlin, thinking "that hurts everyone." Many products specifically made for older people are not bought or used because it's clear they were specifically made for older people, a Catch-22 in which many marketers get caught. (Hearing aids and personal emergency devices are two examples.) Making a product and selling it are two very different things, and many companies don't invest the resources to do the latter well. Only 35% of people 75 or older consider themselves "old," according to Pew Research Center, a fact suggesting that marketing by age is fundamentally misguided. Americans 50 years old and older account for 83% of household wealth, this alone is a reason for marketers to do a much better job creating and promoting products and services that the former will actually want to buy.[30]

Still, marketers in certain industries are licking their chops at the prospect of tens of millions of baby boomers aging in place. The smart home is coming, many futurists are saying, good news for makers of things like technology integrators, smart access controls, and consumer-facing DIY monitoring systems. Telehealth and the ability to remotely track wellness and even a person's activity is expected to be a huge business, not just for the residence market but also for senior housing, assisted living, and memory care centers. Marketers, rather than consumers, are pushing for such technologies, making one wonder if the venture capital being put toward such innovations is well spent.[31]

Those in what is sometimes called "social design" are also excited about the possibilities to create many kinds of products with older people in mind. A telephone with numbers the size of quarters became the poster child of such products, sadly, but designers have thankfully moved beyond that kind of ageist thinking. Internet-connected devices, such as behavioral-based learning thermostats, smartphones with apps to control home appliances, and digital voice assistants are the latest generation of social design. Whether consumers want it or not, building "intelligence" into systems via sensors is likely to be the next wave, allowing family members and caregivers to know whether their loved one or care receiver is sleeping, using the oven, going to the bathroom, or brushing his or her teeth. A notification is sent if there is some kind of unusual activity in behavioral patterns, supposedly offering "peace of mind" for the carer. Nutrition and medication monitoring is part of this approach, a big leap from the "I've-fallen-and-I-can't-get-up" kind of medical alerts.[32]

While staying in one's own home and, if necessary, adapting it to make it age friendlier is often the goal, some older adults are heading to senior cohousing communities (SCCs). Such a living arrangement may be the best option for those who are single and childless or live far away from their families. SCCs are a form of communal living that blends common areas and private residences, a best-of-both-worlds situation for a growing number of older baby boomers. There are currently a few dozen such communities in the United States, but there will likely be many more in the years ahead because they offer independence without the social isolation that often comes with it. SCCs are tribes of a sort, in that they bring together people with shared values, such as environmental sustainability, social justice, or form of spirituality. Residents live in separate homes but share some spaces, such as a common building with a kitchen, library, and exercise room, with patios and gardens designed to promote interaction.[33]

Another interesting model in the communal living space is Silvernest. While it's fundamentally intergenerational, Silvernest's home-sharing concept is especially appealing to older folks who want to cut costs and avoid social isolation. Like SCCs, Silvernest offers both independence and connection, a powerful combination in the emerging longevity economy. Homeowners rent out some extra space in their house or apartment to someone attracted to the idea of having a roommate and saving some money on having one's own place. Through its matchmaking algorithm, much like that of a dating site, Silvernest pairs empty nesters with potential roommates, building in compatibility and safety protocols. Silvernest has seemingly traded on the appeal of the classic TV show *Golden Girls* in building its business model, not at all a bad thing given the (fictionalized) dynamic among the four women of a certain age home sharing in Miami.[34]

Assisted living is now understandably commonly viewed as something to avoid if at all possible, but it will no doubt continue to provide a valuable service for a segment of the older population. Since 2000, A Place for Mom (APFM) has helped millions of families navigate the often difficult process of deciding where to place an aging relative who requires some assistance. As the largest senior living referral service in the country (and Canada), APFM performs many different services to increase the odds that mom (or dad or an uncle or aunt) will be happy where she (or he) lives. APFM is actually a free service (participating communities and partners in its network pay the fee), and there are "caring advisors" charged with finding the best fit for an individual. As they head into their 70s and 80s, boomers will try to retain their independence at all costs (having perhaps visited a parent in an assisted living facility or a nursing home), but the service will remain an important one for those who need (and can afford) it.[35]

The Newest Battlefield

Business opportunity knocks not just in housing but also in virtually every product and service category as the population ages. Marketers are already getting in on the action, fully aware that older consumers may very well represent their largest and wealthiest audience until the mid-21st century. AARP, because of its powerful brand and amazing reach, is likely the premier marketer to older consumers, a position it may hold for some time. A big reason many people join the organization is to receive the discounts that many companies offer to members. (I'm a card-carrying member myself and happily use it whenever I stay at Hampton Inn.) New York Life, Delta Dental, UnitedHealthcare, The Hartford, Goldman Sachs, 1–800-Flowers, Avis, British Airways, Hilton, and Dennys are just a few of the marketers who've partnered with AARP, a smart move given how much business it can generate.

Most marketers, however, remain stuck in a time warp dictating that any consumer who turns 60 resembles Methuselah, the biblical patriarch who lived to age 969. In a 2020 piece for the *Harvard Business Review*, Vaughan Emsley tells how right after he became a sexagenarian, he became the target of online and print advertisers selling products and services such as incontinence, erectile dysfunction, and burial (the latter via a direct mail piece from a cemetery). Emsley had not searched online for any of these things, making him conclude that the advertisers found him just by his age. A decline in health and looming death seemed to be how marketers characterized the state of 60-somethings, a strange and disturbing thing. "Meanwhile, I've seen virtually no marketing for the kinds of things I'm interested in, such as great hotels in Rome or beautiful places to hike in upstate New York," Emsley remarked, capturing marketers' age-myopia in a nutshell.[36]

Emsley, a cofounder of the consultancy Flipside, went on to cite figures regarding the frequency of negative portrayals of older people in advertising (28%) and how often they are shown in isolated situations (70%!). Older adults were rarely included in online advertising, an AARP study had found and, when they were, a medical professional was often nearby. One certainly wouldn't know that Americans over age 50 accounted for more than half of consumer spending in the United States, a fact made even more remarkable in that just an estimated 5% to 10% of marketing budgets were devoted to that group. The 50+ segment is forecast to grow 34% through 2030, according to Nielsen, yet more reason it's time that businesspeople got over their ageist thinking and started treating people equally.[37] Jeff Weiss, CEO of the consultancy Age of Majority, believes that millennials' fear of getting older is behind their reluctance to market to older consumers, an interesting take on the situation.[38]

Not helping matters are all the ads for "smart pills," i.e., over-the-counter performance-and-image enhancing drugs (PIED) that promise to improve memory or cognition or even slow the onset of dementia. "There are no pills that have such dramatic effects," flatly states Harriet Hall, MD, in *Skeptical Inquirer* in 2020, dismissive of such things whether they're called smart drugs, cognitive enhancers, or nootropics. Some ads claim that said product is "pharmacist recommended," a complete fabrication given that no pharmacist would advise taking the drugs. One claim made by Procera AVH is that it "revitalizes tired, sluggish brain cells with a fresh supply of oxygen and key vital nutrients," sounding much like the miracle tonics sold in the 19th century. The Federal Trade Commission and state attorney generals are going after some of these advertisers, but *caveat emptor* should be the rule for such products. Besides being a waste of money and potentially harmful, the promotion of smart pills makes it appear that much or most of the primary target audience—older people—have poor memory and thinking skills, which is not true. The only thing of which PIED can be said to be effective is the spread of ageism.[39]

The ubiquity of advertising for prescription medication can also be interpreted as ageist. Steve Johnson, an upstate New York communications expert, has noted that people of age make frequent appearances in pharmaceutical commercials but not much else of the advertising landscape. The impression this leaves with viewers is that, more than anything else, older adults have all kinds of medical problems that should be treated, even at the risk of all the side effects mentioned in the ads. In place of this unhealthy image, Johnson suggests, why don't advertisers adopt a more accurate characterization of the group, one defined by experience. Should one have to choose a single word, experience is indeed the best descriptor of an older person, if only because he or she has lived more years than younger people. Experience is a good thing, anyone who possesses it will tell you, a primary agent of happiness and resiliency. "The loss-oriented language associated with the second half of life—'retirement,' 'empty nest,' 'downsizing'—is particularly in need of a rethink," Johnson noted, with experience the key to changing the narrative of aging from a negative perspective to a positive one.[40]

Nancy Trent, the head of a wellness public relations firm specializing in the cosmetics industry, sees only an upside in marketers taking a more positive view of older consumers. Trent calls the cohort (made up of baby boomers and older Gen Xers) Generation Silver (or just Gen S), reflecting not just the typical hair color of the market but also the fact that it has by far the most disposable income of any. (Eighty percent of them are even covering at least some of the expenses of their adult children, according to NerdWallet.) "Aging is coming back in fashion," Trent stated in 2020, thinking that Generation S will serve as "influencers" because of their great numbers and immense spending power.[41] Not just cosmetics but fashion too seems to be warming up to the silver market. "Perceptions about what's 'age-appropriate' are shifting as designers, retailers, and celebrities like Heidi Klum (47), Jennifer Lopez (51), Halle Berry (54), and Angela Bassett (62) are encouraging a rejuvenated approach to fashion," a 2020 article in *O: The Oprah Magazine*, read, happy to report that "these days, women are proving that getting older and looking better than ever go hand in hand."[42]

The appearance associated with aging does indeed appear to be becoming more fashionable. Cosmetics marketers around the world have historically focused on the youth market but now are increasingly shifting their attention to older consumers as the global population ages. While "reverse aging" is a ridiculous, oxymoronic concept, there's nothing of course wrong with using a product that can enhance one's appearance. The market for makeup, lotions, lipsticks, and foundations is growing fast as older consumers buy products that have been produced with their bodies in mind. As *Allure*'s bold stance against "anti-aging" suggests, the emerging narrative of beauty is less about hiding the "bad" and more about bringing out the "good." Shiseido is one company going after the 50+ market, having created a dedicated line of products under the brand name Prior. Yuki Kawai, the brand manager of Prior, says the question that should be asked (by anyone) is, "What's beautiful about my age?", an excellent example of age-friendly marketing.[43]

Also expressing considerable friendship toward baby boomers these days is Facebook. Boomers use all kinds of social media but do like Facebook a lot, replacing many younger users who've moved on to cooler, more video-oriented Instagram (which Facebook owns), Snapchat, and TikTok. COVID-19 accelerated boomers' reliance on online technology for work, shopping, and socializing, good news for Facebook as it tries to attract new users and heavier traffic to support its advertising model. Facebook has recently pitched ad agencies on having their clients target the boomer market, a refreshing change of pace given most marketers' reluctance to do so. There's some irony that it is a social media company founded and still run by hoodie-wearing 20-somethings who recognize the opportunity of "Generation S."[44]

As Facebook learned, the stereotype of older people being online challenged just isn't true. Even before the spread of COVID-19 and Zooming of the world, the online habits of older people were not much different from those of Gen X, millennials, and even Gen Z. That's what Boston Digital, a digital marketing agency found in a 2020 survey. The percentage of people in each age cohort who shopped or socialized online shopping and social media was remarkably consistent, more reason why boomer consumers should not be viewed by marketers as technological dumbbells. "Businesses can't afford to base their marketing strategies on outdated ideas of how age groups behave," said Peter Prodromou, president of Boston Digital, in reporting the results of the survey. "We're no longer completely siloed generations," he added, thinking that "companies need to bake this reality into their marketing strategies."[45]

As it did for all for us, COVID-19 altered many of the ways that older people got things done, a direct result of the inability to go out into the real world. It also proved that "mature" consumers were much more flexible than marketers had thought, meaning they were open to exploring new product categories and using different brands. Switching brands if the preferred one was out of stock was not a problem for older folks, it turned out, throwing a monkey wrench into the commonly accepted tenet that 60- and 70-somethings were irrevocably stuck in their ways. "Older consumers age 55 and up, previously known for being intensely brand loyal, are now in play," wrote Adrienne Pasquarelli for *Advertising Age* in 2020, declaring that "senior shoppers are the newest battlefield." Shifting from brick-and-mortar shopping to online shopping has been another way that older consumers have proved they are not much different from younger generations (except for having a lot more money).[46]

Even if older consumers are increasingly in play, it's difficult for marketers, most of whom are millennials and Gen Z, to not subscribe to ageist thinking, as it's thoroughly woven into everyday life. Ageist thinking prescribes a marketing approach steeped in a consciousness of age and specifically negative feelings about older age. Such profiling is both silly and discriminatory, and not any different from marketers defining consumers as black or women or gay or physically impaired in some way. We're all just people and want to be thought of that way, without the demographic and social divisions that separate us. Tapping into universal and positive human values (love, community, empathy, purpose in life, the desire to express one's voice) is a far better approach than one shaped by a person's age (or race or gender).

Baby boomers will thus be most attracted to those brands that do not define the group or individuals in terms of age, especially older age. They will prefer those brands that reinforce the idea that boomers are essentially the same people they used to be when they were younger, except that they now have a broader perspective from having spent more years on the planet. Defining brands in generational terms is just as divisive and limiting as defining them by race or gender. Should a marketer decide to consciously address baby boomers, I'd recommend messaging that celebrates their proud past, recognizes their meaningful and purposeful present, and anticipates their still relevant future.

Are any marketers getting it right? Happily, yes. Those who are finding success in "the newest battlefield" understand that the tens of millions of baby boomers are not yesterday's news but in fact tomorrow's and are eager to establish relationships with them. Apple, for example, has shown it understands the obvious but often overlooked fact that segmenting an audience based on biological traits is both silly and divisive. In the company's "Behind the Mac-Greatness" commercial, people of all ages, colors, and walks of life, famous and otherwise, use their Macs to pursue their particular passion, age friendliness at its best.

Another company that clearly gets it is Omaha-based Home Instead Senior Care, which offers "personalized care services for those who choose to age happily at home." Beyond being in a future-proof business (we all eventually get old), Home Instead is fully committed to a truly diverse and inclusive workforce. Age often gets lost in corporate diversity and inclusion initiatives, taking a back seat to addressing inequalities based on race and gender, but some of Home Instead's caregivers are in their 80s and 90s!

One doesn't have to work for a major company to be an age-friendly marketer. Pickleball, a cross among badminton, tennis, and table tennis played on a smaller court within a regulation size tennis court, is reportedly America's fastest-growing sport. The number of people playing Pickleball is rising fast and will continually do so as millions more folks—especially older ones—look for a sport that requires considerable moving around, sharp reflexes, and good balance and agility but with a low risk of injury. Smart managers of public parks, rec centers, and clubs are capitalizing on the trend by reconfiguring tennis courts, showing that age friendliness can happen anytime and anywhere.

Boomers 3.0

In my *Boomers 3.0: Marketing to Baby Boomers in Their Third Act of Life*, I outlined ten strategies that businesspeople should consider when marketing to older consumers. These strategies were grounded in what I believed to be the core values of Americans in the third act of life—i.e., baby boomers—and were thus a reflection of the individual and collective DNA that guided their attitudes and behavior. As cultural indicators of how older consumers are likely to spend their time and money, I saw these ten strategies as territories for marketers to stake and mine with products, services, and communications. Although this is not a how-to book per se, it would be a missed opportunity not to offer a brief overview of them as a platform for age-friendly marketing.[47]

The first strategy, "Forever Young," made the case that much like still active 70-something musicians including Paul McCartney, Rod Stewart, Tina Turner, Neil Diamond, Paul Simon, and the "Strolling Bones," many baby boomers are displaying clear signs of what is considered youthfulness. Although one's body may not have got the memo, youth is not something that necessarily goes away at age 20, 30, or any other chronological measure; rather, youthfulness is an idea that anyone, regardless of his or her age, can subscribe to as part of an approach to or philosophy of life. This is especially true for boomers, who broke away from their parents' generation by adopting a lifestyle and political orienta-tion that immediately became associated with youthful values. A half-century and change after the counterculture, many boomers continue to hold onto their determination to think, act, and appear young, making this good strategic fod-der for marketers.[48]

The second strategy, "Old Dog, New Tricks," showed how many of those in the third act of life are pursuing knowledge of all kinds. It's clear that old dogs are indeed capable of learning new tricks, as baby boomers satisfy their thirst to know more about some aspect of the world for professional or personal reasons. Boomers' expansion of their gray matter is grounded in research dispel-ling the myth that cognition declines with age; study after study has shown that the human brain continues to generate new cells as it ages. Research also sug-gests that older brains do best when exposed to intellectual stimuli, making the idea of use-it-or-lose-it especially true for aging cerebral cortexes. Fortunately, as the most highly educated generation in history (until millennials came along), boomers are very interested in continuing to learn and try new things and will remain curious about the world throughout their third act. Businesses should leverage older dogs' wish to learn new tricks, I advised, another example of age-friendly marketing.[49]

The third strategy, "Reboot," argued that older people are entirely capable of reinventing themselves in some way. Contrary to popular belief, baby boomers are just as amenable to making major life changes when situations call for them, whether they involve work, relationships, where to live, romance, or spiritual-ity. Whether carefully planned out or serendipitous, rebooting is about looking forward rather than backward, challenging the idea that older adults spend most of their time remembering better days when they were young. Popular culture about baby boomers is overly nostalgic, making it seem like they represent a chapter in American history rather than a group of people who are still leading active, interesting lives. While it's true that many boomers are not reluctant to tell their kids about how they got arrested at a sit-in to protest the Vietnam War, stayed up super late to see the first men walk on the moon (I did), or saw Led Zeppelin on their first North American concert tour, we're actually more interested in what lies ahead in the future than in what happened in the past. Think of boomers as a work in progress open to new experiences, I recommended; this too is entirely consistent with age-friendly marketing.[50]

The fourth strategy, "Inner Muse," detailed how there is an intimate relationship between baby boomers and creativity, one that will no doubt continue to blossom. Research shows that creativity helps midlifers and older people stay engaged and feel good about themselves and serves as a prime way for them to remain optimistic and excited about life. Fortunately, boomers have been steeped in creativity throughout their lives, with aesthetics viewed as an essential way to express one's individuality. Given all this, finding one's inner muse—the goddess of art—will be a primary pursuit of boomers through their third act, I believe, particularly because many have the time and money to nurture a particular avenue of creativity. Surf the wave of boomer creativity as they age, I told readers, an expression of age friendliness.[51]

The fifth strategy, "Bucket List," pointed out how many baby boomers are writing bucket lists, i.e., an inventory of desired experiences in life that an individual did not get around to completing because he or she did not have the time, money, or initiative. By the third act of life, however, such a list looms large in the minds of many, as the recognition that one will run out of time at some point in the future becomes more real. Boomers are now heavily investing in bucket lists, sometimes literally so, with many more inventories of must-do-before-I-die experiences to be taken in the years ahead. The world is a very big place with an incredible array of things to see and do, after all, but most of us live relatively narrow lives for most of our lives. A bucket list is a rare opportunity to step out of our little box and, as they say, better late than never. Whatever the pursuit, marketers of all sorts have a golden opportunity to be part of this existential free-for-all, making the offering of once-in-a-lifetime experience reflective of age friendliness.[52]

The sixth strategy, "Higher Ground," described the evolution of human beings in their third act of life, a concept that many baby boomers have embraced. Metaphorically reaching for higher ground is about the big stuff of life—gaining experience and wisdom, realizing one's full potential, advancing one's spirituality, and, perhaps most important, embracing aging. The ability to do this is in some respects a function of the peace of mind many boomers are beginning to experience as they head through their 60s and 70s. There is a common belief among many of them that one is now playing with house money, meaning they feel they have already lived a full life and anything good that happens to them at this point is a bonus. Every day is a gift to be appreciated and savored, they can say in all honesty, a wonderful luxury to be able to possess. The physical signs of aging are offset by an accumulation of personal growth and wisdom, I can personally attest, a function of life experience and a greater awareness of one's own mortality.[53]

Research does indeed show that aging does often bring a greater sense of well-being and emotional contentedness, with the demons of youth mostly gone and the compulsions of both id and ego mostly sated. Older people are slower to get angry and are more likely to see the bright side of complicated situations, studies also have revealed, with conflict-solving another skill acquired through experience. As well, boomers are prone to forgive and forget when things go south in a relationship, a reflection of their ability to see the bigger picture. Marketers can put this powerful idea into action by reinforcing the fact that the third act of life is the ideal time to experience a different level of joy and to realize one's full potential. Defining a brand as an agent of higher ground, in other words, is a prime way to be age friendly.[54]

The seventh strategy, "Boomerpods," put forth the notion that community has always been an essential strand in baby boomers' DNA, an attribute that will serve them well in their later years. Boomers' natural leaning to create communities is in part a function of their being what was the biggest community in history; the group became recognized as a distinct generation or "cohort" as soon as they were born after World War II. Boomers (and marketers) learned quickly there is power in numbers, something that still holds true today despite the media's (and marketers', ironically) fascination with millennials and Gen Z. With many boomers now empty nesters, their desire to get together with people who share something in common is arguably stronger than ever. While many such communities are somehow rooted in the past—there is currently a deep desire among boomers to reconnect with people who were once important in their lives—they are not just looking back but forward. Boomers are keen on forming new kinds of connections, friendships, and alliances, strengthening the role of community in their lives.[55]

The appeal of "Boomerpods"—my term for close-knit communities shared by baby boomers and characterized by strong personal or professional affiliations—is backed up by studies indicating that belonging to a social network is good for older people's minds and bodies. It is vital to be around other people, in other words, especially later in life. Boomerpods will become more important in the years ahead as American society further fragments, I believe, with groups of people having something in common banding together in an increasingly diverse country and world. For marketers of all kinds, the concept of Boomerpods is obviously an important one, as a synergy often results when people get together.

Whatever comes out of a collective group is almost always greater than the sum of its individual parts, in other words, making the plugging into existing and emerging communities an avenue leading toward age friendliness.[56]

The eighth strategy, "Gray Power," riffed on the Black Power movement of the late 1960s, when more militant African Americans formed an ideology based on forceful activism and empowerment. Baby boomers are now becoming a recognized constituency in their third act of life, building on the efforts of seniors of past generations who made their presence known in order to shape public policy. The political clout of boomers will further coalesce in the years ahead if only because the group represents a major voting bloc for any elected official or candidate regardless of party. Boomers will exert great influence on the nation's political and economic landscape, I believe, seeing the effort as their last opportunity to shape the country's future. Combatting ageism will be part of this activism, naturally, centered on giving older people the respect and fair treatment they deserve. Gray Power is thus analogous in some respects to previous large-scale movements by marginalized groups, e.g., civil rights, feminism, and gay rights. Aligning with boomers as their power consolidates over the next two decades is a smart strategy for virtually any kind of business, I suggested, making Gray Power a vehicle of age-friendly marketing.[57]

The ninth strategy, "Pay It Forward," was about baby boomers' "deep-seated desire to make a difference," as Dan Kadlec, coauthor of *A New Purpose*, described it. Giving back is already becoming a principal activity among boomers, specifically some form of passing on what one has learned in life so far. Offering expertise in a particular area to a younger generation or others in need can be an immensely rewarding experience and lead to a feeling of completion or coming full circle. Paying it forward will become much more structured and organized in the years ahead, I foresee, with millions of boomers looking for a new mission in life offering meaning and purpose. (There actually may be a biological component to the urge to pay it forward; some of the greatest psychologists of the 20th century, including Abraham Maslow and Eric Erikson, have argued that humans are hardwired to give back in their later years, part of the evolutionary process.) Taking the initiative by creating opportunities by which boomers can pay it forward would be a wise move for organizations, I opined, a win-win example of age friendliness.[58]

The final strategy I included in *Boomers 3.0* was "Footprints-in-the-Sand," the desire to leave something behind after one is gone. Creating some form of legacy is top of mind for many baby boomers, as more and more ask themselves, "How can or will I be remembered?" It is difficult to overestimate boomers' interest in making others know that they spent some time on Earth, in the process realizing a kind of immortality. Giving money and/or time to a cause in which one believes also happens to be a good way for an older person to become less depressed, have lower blood pressure, and live longer. Many studies show that giving and volunteering are good for one's health, as being generous is an important source of happiness for those who choose to do it. Older givers are not just happier and healthier than nongivers but also have a stronger sense of purpose and higher self-esteem, more reason to be excited about the philanthropic windfall that is looming as baby boomers age. It turns out that helping people in need offers a greater opportunity to find joy in life than spending money on oneself, something that perhaps should make all of us question our priorities. Need it be said, this is a highly valuable pursuit, and I urged that businesses find ways to help boomers leave their footprints in the sand. Can there be a better illustration of age-friendly marketing?[59]

Notes

1 "More Seniors Seek Marijuana for Age-related Ailments," *Long Island Business News* March 25, 2019.

2 Peter Hubbell, *The Old Rush: Marketing for Gold in the Age of Aging* (Greenwich, CT: LID Publishing, 2014).

3 Peter Hubbell, *Getting Better with Age: Improving Marketing in the Age of Aging* (Greenwich, CT: LID Publishing, 2015).

4 Lawrence R. Samuel, *Boomers 3.0: Marketing to Baby Boomers in Their Third Act of Life* (Santa Barbara, CA: Prager, 2017).

5 Joseph F. Coughlin, *The Longevity Economy: Unlocking the World's Fastest-Growing, Most Misunderstood Market* (New York: Public Affairs, 2017).

6 *The Longevity Economy* 22.

7 James H. Johnson, Jr., Allan M. Parnell, and Huan Lian, "Aging as an Engine of Innovation, Business Development, and Employment Growth," *Economic Development Journal*, Summer 2018, 32.

8 "Aging as an Engine of Innovation, Business Development, and Employment Growth," 32.

9 Ken Dychtwald and Robert Morison, *What Retirees Want: A Holistic View of Life's Third Age* (Hoboken, NJ: Wiley, 2020) 5.

10 *What Retirees Want*.

11 Ian Sohn, "Over the Advertising Hill," *Adweek*, February 10, 2020, 10.

12 Tiffany Hsu, "Older People Are Ignored and Distorted in Ageist Marketing, Report Finds," *New York Times (Online)*, September 23, 2019.

13 "Disrupt Aging: Reinventing What It Means to Age," aarp.org.

14 Kindra Cooper, "AARP and Refinery29 Take on Ageism in the Advertising Industry," *customercontactweekdigital.com*, May 29, 2019.

15 Andrea Felsted, "Boomers Are Going to Drive a Silver Surge," *Bloomberg.com*, January 29, 2021.

16 AARP, "The Longevity Economy Outlook," 7.

17 Ben Steverman, "Boomers Are Thriving on an 'Unprecedented' 9 Trillion Inheritance," *Bloomberg.com*, November 19, 2019.

18 "Boomers Are Thriving on an 'Unprecedented' $9 Trillion Inheritance."

19 Lananh Nguyen, "U.S. Women's Control of $10 Trillion Set to Triple in a Decade," *Bloomberg.com*, July 29, 2020.

20 "Aging Is an Opportunity," globalcoalitiononaging.com.

21 globalcoalitiononaging.com.

22 globalcoalitiononaging.com.

23 Susan Wilner Golden and Laura Carstensen, "How Merrill Lynch Is Planning for Its Customers to Live to 100," *Harvard Business Review*, March 4, 2019.

24 Michael Klowden and Paul Irving, "From the CEO," *The Milken Institute Review: A Journal of Economic Policy*, January 2020, 1a.

25 silverdisobedience.rocks.

26 Michael Tobin, "The VCs Betting on Aging Consumers," *Bloomberg Businessweek*, August 3, 2020.

27 "Two Thought Leaders in the Longevity Economy and Life Sciences Partner for a Series of Events Focused on Early-Stage Investment in Health and Innovation for People Ages 50+," *PR Newswire US*, January 7, 2021.

28 Fran O'Brien, "Protecting Assets When Clients Age in Place," *Investment Advisor*, June 2019, 48.

29 "Protecting Assets When Clients Age in Place."

30 Joseph F. Coughlin, "How 'Old Age' Was Invented—and Why It Needs to be Reinvented," *MIT Technology Review*, September/October 2019, 34.

31 Silvia Madrigal, "Healthcare: Riding the Age Wave," *Security Business*, February 2019.

32 Lou Lenzi, "Social Design: From Universal Design to Eldercare Services," *Appliance Design*, June 2018, 40.

33 Nancy Kropis and Sherry Cummings, "Older Baby Boomers Create Living Arrangements to Suit New Needs," *New Orleans CityBusiness*, September 11, 2019.

34 silvernest.com.

35 aplaceformom.com.

36 Vaughan Emsley, "Don't Estimate the Market Power of the 50+ Crowd," *Harvard Business Review*, January 9, 2020.

37 "Don't Estimate the Market Power of the 50+ Crowd."

38 Adrienne Pasquarelli, "Senior Shoppers Are the Newest Battlefield," *Advertising Age*, October 19, 2020.

39 Harriet Hall, "Smart Pills? Beware the PIED Piper," *Skeptical Inquirer*, January–February 2020, 19.

40 Steve Johnson, "Rx for Marketing to Older, Wiser Consumers," *Business Journal (Central New York)*, August 6, 2018, 11.

41 Nancy Trent, "5 R's of Generation Silver," *Global Cosmetic Industry*, July/August 2020, 41–42.

42 "Fashion Comes of Age," *O: The Oprah Magazine*, November 2020.

43 James E. Ellis, "Old Age Could Be a Beauty Gold Mine," *Bloomberg Businessweek*, December 9, 2019, 16–17.

44 Garett Sloane, "How Facebook Is Helping Brands Capture Boomer Dollars," *Advertising Age*, October 19, 2020.

45 "Older Consumers Conduct Significant Portions of Daily Life Online, Just Like Younger Ones, Finds New Survey by Boston Digital," *PR Newswire US*, April 22, 2020.

46 "Senior Shoppers Are the Newest Battlefield."

47 *Boomers 3.0.*

48 *Boomers 3.0.*

49 *Boomers 3.0.*

50 *Boomers 3.0.*

51 *Boomers 3.0.*

52 *Boomers 3.0.*

53 *Boomers 3.0.*

54 *Boomers 3.0.*

55 *Boomers 3.0.*

56 *Boomers 3.0.*

57 *Boomers 3.0.*

58 *Boomers 3.0.*

59 *Boomers 3.0.*

Chapter 5

Age-Friendly Responsibility

Good is the new cool.

Afdhel Aziz
Social entrepreneur, 2019

In September 1970, the economist Milton Friedman published an essay in the *New York Times Magazine* that was widely received as a manifesto for free-market capitalism. In his "The Social Responsibility of Business Is to Increase Its Profits," Friedman, who had achieved celebrity status by his regular appearances on television talk shows, made the convincing case that corporations' only job was to make money for itself and its shareholders. Greed was good for everybody, the essay implied, with any social good to trickle down from those who financially benefited from corporate avarice.[1]

A half-century later, the "essay heard round the world," as the same publication called it, was deemed as obsolete as a Ford Pinto. CEOs of major corporations, university professors, contemporary economists, and other pundits were invited to offer their thoughts on the piece against the backdrop of the much different business climate that had emerged over the past generation. "The decades since have only exposed his [Friedman's] myopia," Marc Benioff of Salesforce commented, a sentiment that most of the contributors expressed in some way or another.[2]

What had happened to turn Friedman's classic work from a road map for businesses to follow into a danger zone to avoid at all costs? Three words:

corporate social responsibility (CSR). CSR is among the most popular pursuits in business today, a very good thing toward achieving a more age-friendly society. The goals of CSR are in fact ideally aligned with the principles of age friendliness, reason to be optimistic that older people in America have a chance of being treated equitably. With businesses taking social responsibility seriously, discrimination against any group will, at least in theory, not be tolerated by employees, consumers, and investors, something that bodes well for ending ageism once and for all. Within the diversity and inclusion universe, race and gender have led the way, and now business is increasingly supporting the rights of the disability and LGBTQ communities. Similar action needs to be taken with regard to older workers, consumers, and citizens if equality is to be realized. Businesspeople of all levels should think about how to apply some of the ideas of age-friendly communities, age-friendly work, and age-friendly marketing laid out in previous chapters of this book into their CSR plans and programs, finding them to be complementary and synergistic.

The Beating Heart

In their 2020 *The Corporate Social Mind: How Companies Lead Social Change from the Inside Out*, Derrick Feldmann and Michael Alberg-Seberich made a convincing case that companies now have the opportunity and responsibility to do much more than sell things to us. "Companies can be the beating heart behind so many of our issues today—if they choose to be," they wrote, thinking that "our combined voices can truly move society toward change." Corporate citizenship has evolved from a philanthropy model to one based in societal impact, the authors suggest, the latter a holistic approach that leverages an organization's assets. "Companies that make a conscious decision to infuse the good of society into their business do so in an effort to make business and society work together in a symbiotic relationship to fulfill the needs of individuals, families, and the places we call home," Feldmann and Alberg-Seberich stated, this their titular "corporate social mind."[3]

In his 2020 *Elevated Economics: How Conscious Consumers Will Fuel the Future of Business*, Richard Steel posited that a new "P" has recently been added to the classic "4Ps" of business (product, price, place, promotion): purpose. Consumers and shareholders have moved ahead of companies in terms of the role that business should play in society, he believed, his "elevated economics" essentially equivalent to conscious capitalism. "Our economy has become increasingly value-driven," he wrote, "and consumers have begun to care more about the principles of the companies from which they buy." CSR and impact investing are not just trends but emblematic of where business is heading, Steel advised, this turning point in capitalism a call to action for forward-thinking companies.[4]

With social activism in the air, CSR has become a go-theme among journalists covering the business beat. "It's often not enough to sell a product or service," noted Deborah Capras in *Business Spotlight* in 2020, thinking that "today, businesses need to be about something bigger." Making the world better in some way is the goal, although some companies in certain businesses settle for just trying to not make it worse. CSR can be viewed as a confluence of doing what's best for the company, as well as for society. Attracting customers and making employees feel pride in their jobs are key reasons to adopt CSR as an initiative, although the concept is intended to stretch well beyond those factors. As a kind of cousin to CSR, ESG (environmental, social, and governance) offers investors the opportunity to put their money in companies that focus not just on financial performance. Such investors choose companies that are ethical, transparent in their business operations, and engage in no activities that have a negative effect on people or the environment.[5]

Because it directly relates to age-friendly CSR, a primer on ESG would be helpful. The E in ESG stands for environmental criteria, including the energy a company consumes, the waste it discharges, and the resources it uses. A company's relative "carbon footprint" is often the focus of the E component of ESG. S is for social criteria, meaning the relationships in the company and the reputation it has within the communities it does business with. Labor relations and diversity and inclusion are central to S. G represents governance, i.e., the internal system of practices, controls, and procedures that a company employs to manage itself, make decisions, comply with laws, and satisfy external stakeholders. Age-friendly responsibility falls mostly into the social category, but governance, too, plays an important role in the lives of older workers.[6]

It wasn't surprising that both *The Corporate Social Mind* and *Elevated Economics* were from the same publisher—Fast Company Press. In 1995, the first issue of *Fast Company* magazine appeared, offering a much different kind of take on business than its official, century-old voice, the *Wall Street Journal.* "We want to shape the conversation about business at its best and the real meaning of success," editors Bill Taylor and Alan Webber wrote in the premiere issue; their view of capitalism was a lot broader than how much money a company was making for itself and its shareholders. For the next quarter-century, *Fast Company* blazed a new trail within the media landscape, offering a more humanistic and socially conscious view of the business scene. In 2020, *Fast Company* issued its "New Rules of Business," a manifesto of sorts that urged companies to embed humane values, innovation, and corporate responsibility into their respective vision and mission.[7]

Much of the world has caught up with *Fast Company*'s bold break from literally business as usual. Today, in our activist social climate, capitalism is under pressure to do more than maximize short-term profits. This is a good thing, needless to say, especially for older people who've been marginalized and disenfranchised by Corporate America as both workers and consumers. Baking social responsibility into an organization's culture can be a challenging thing, however, as most companies were not founded with social purpose in mind. (Whole Foods and TOMS Shoes are notable exceptions.) And if a company is doing well, why should it change horses in midstream? Giving away money would be an easy thing to do and perhaps make top executives (and the donees) happy but changing the way companies actually make money offers a much more sustainable proposition. Indra K. Nooyi, who worked with PepsiCo in this area as a consultant, calls such an approach "Performance with Purpose," with financial, human, environmental, and talent sustainability all part of the mix.[8]

Such an approach is far better than what is known as "woke capitalism," in which businesses respond to a social issue (such as racism) through corporate messaging or strategic philanthropy. As Nooyi makes clear, sustainability is the key to social responsibility, as only this is capable of creating goodwill among all stakeholders over the long term. Patagonia and Ben & Jerry's are two companies that have over the course of decades shown genuine caring toward their employees and communities through policies and practices. Not surprisingly, both of these companies are certified B Corporations, meaning they have met certain criteria for corporate transparency, worker benefits, and energy efficiency (as set by the nonprofit B Lab) and that they are accountable to a wide range of stakeholders (versus shareholders).[9]

It's not an overstatement to say that B Lab, a nonprofit that is dedicated to the idea that business must be a force for good, has the potential to transform the global economy. Tens of thousands of companies around the world have been certified as a B (as in Benefit) Corporation, i.e., one committed to creating positive social results, as well as financial ones. Such companies are for-profits, it should be noted, the difference being that the leaders of B Corps are interested in driving change, as well as making money. Whether or not they have been certified as such, companies big and small have used CSR strategies to increase shareholder value while serving the public in some way. The dream of those who subscribe to the business-as-a-force-for-good is a "benefit" economy in which financial goals and social purpose are seamlessly combined, quite a grand vision.[10]

While social responsibility has gained traction through the 21st century (running parallel with the aging of America and the world, it should be noted), the COVID-19 pandemic directed it into a new trajectory. Susan McPherson, considered to be a "guru" in the CSR field, believes that the pandemic elevated corporate social responsibility from a "nice to have" to a core business strategy. "COVID will demand a fundamental reset in how business interacts with society and its resources, from paying taxes to funding health care to providing training and employment opportunities for marginalized communities," she told *Newsweek* in 2020, urging CEOs to "reimagine what a new future can look like." Everyone—employees, customers, investors, and communities—benefits when companies step up, according to McPherson, making a strong case for "purpose-driven brands."[11]

In their 2020 article for *Harvard Business Review* titled "What Good Business Looks Like," Paul Polman, Raj Sisodia, and Kip Tindell agreed that the pandemic was a turning point not just in the history of CSR but also in business itself. Milton Friedman's profits-first-and-only philosophy reflected and shaped the ways in which generations of businesspeople made decisions, but that era was now ending or already over. (His view is credited with having laid the groundwork for the scorch-the-earth brand of capitalism of the 1980s.) Although the rise of the conscious capitalism movement chipped away at that doctrine in the 1990s and early 2000s, the 2020 pandemic smashed it into little bits. "This pandemic is turning out to be a grim but vital reminder that we human beings are here on this planet to take care of each other," the three wrote, believing that "business is a way we can do that at scale." Capitalism is hardly a perfect system, they conceded, but it represents our most effective means of creating positive change. "When the private sector pivots to serve the greater good, its reach and power is immense," they concluded, seeing much upside in this regard as a result of the global crisis.[12]

A Responsibility Revolution

The purposeful augmenting of free-market capitalism with social responsibility has represented a major shift in economic theory. Ever since Adam Smith introduced the concept of the "invisible hand" in his 1759 *The Theory of Moral Sentiments*, it had been generally accepted that the public good would be best served by individuals acting in their own self-interests. All boats would be lifted by such an approach, in other words, helping spread *laissez-faire* ideology (and fuel the Industrial Revolution) for the next couple of centuries, at least in Western societies. Corporate philanthropy grew in the 20th century, particularly in concert with the Great Society programs of the 1960s, but it took a few more decades for the notion of sustainability to work its way into business culture. A big debt can be paid to the economist Margaret M. Blair, whose 1995 *Ownership and Control: Rethinking Corporate Governance for the Twenty-First Century* argued that corporations could maximize their wealth by being responsible not just to shareholders but also stakeholders, such as employees, customers, and communities.[13] Alongside the setting up of foundations for nonprofits, many companies are now serving as advocates for particular issues, making Smith's hand entirely visible.[14]

With a broad definition of sustainability now sweeping through the business world, virtually all elements of an organization are being reevaluated. A food company is likely to consider how to use organic, locally sourced ingredients to make its products and then decide to kick in a percentage of sales to environmental causes. But the idea of sustainability can go far beyond such initiatives by "greening" the organization itself. Committing to a diverse workforce—and yes, including employees' age—can be interpreted as greening, as could offering health insurance and retirements to all employees. "Welcome to the new green, one that requires even the most thoughtful businesses to not only rethink sustainability but to redefine what they—and their shareholders and investors—think of as success," Erika Bolstad wrote in *Oregon Business Magazine* in 2019. "Green" has in effect become equivalent to corporate citizenship, i.e., the premise that businesses have a responsibility to people both inside and outside the organization. This is encouraging, needless to say, and a clear sign that business has evolved dramatically over the past generation.[15]

Max H. Bazerman, a professor at the Harvard Business School and the author of *Better, Not Perfect: A Realist's Guide to Maximum Sustainable Goodness*, makes the important point that while companies can and should be socially responsible, it's really up to individuals in positions of power to lead the way. It's great for C-suite executives to be ethical people, of course, but they have the ability to affect the behavior of their whole organization. "Because they are responsible for the decisions of others as well as their own, they can dramatically multiply the amount of good they do by encouraging others to be better," Bazerman wrote in the *Harvard Business Review* in 2020, suggesting that leaders consider how they can shape the perspective of colleagues and their company's decision-making process. "People follow the behavior of others, particularly those in positions of power and prestige," he added, believing that "employees in organizations with ethical leaders can be expected to behave more ethically themselves."[16]

The positive changes currently taking place in Corporate America that promise to lead to an age-friendlier society are seismic in scope. "Business is in the midst of a responsibility revolution," declared O. K. Carter in the *Fort Worth Business Press*, its power demonstrated by the breadth and diversity of the people who and organizations that are supporting it. That greater social responsibility can be good for both business and communities appears to be a no-lose proposition, making it understandable how and why it is supplementing if not replacing the corporate philanthropy model. Grounded in strategy and aimed toward purpose and impact, CSR fits nicely into the planning- and deliverables-intensive approach that most Big Businesses take.[17]

Effectively forced to take social responsibility into account, many corporations that had moved beyond Friedman's philosophy by adding "do no harm" and serving customers to their business mix were now taking an even broader view of the role they should play within society. Social responsibility and social media go hand in hand; it's not surprising that the rise of the former these past two decades has run on a parallel course with that of the latter. Consumers today simply have more power than they used to, as the ability to reach like-minded folks is easier than ever. The balance between company and consumer has irrevocably shifted, a rather rude surprise to organizations resistant to change. "Corporations will increasingly be expected to leverage their strengths in ways that help resolve a host of global issues ranging from human rights, health, and food production to housing, global warming, transportation, water supplies, education and more," Carter thought, a list that should include taking an intergenerational view of workers and consumers.[18]

Now that power belongs to the people (or more that people have realized they hold the power), companies have to acknowledge social responsibility, whether they want to or not. Governments have proved to be remarkably ineffective in addressing social change, encouraging citizens to look to business to get involved. Historically, companies have tried to avoid taking any kind of stance that could be construed as political but, given the rise of "woke capitalism" and its ideological kin, those days are over. It's now impossible to keep the real world out of business, as both consumers and employees are ready, willing, and able to take action should they believe it is warranted. Negative repercussions such as boycotts and walkouts are just a couple of actions consumers and employees can take, effectively forcing companies to embed CSR into their strategic vision. More importantly, however, it is the opportunity that social responsibility presents that should motivate Big Business to build purpose into their plans. It is an ideal time to bring Corporate America's attention to the social and economic calamity that is ageism and reframe global aging as a potentially huge economic opportunity.[19]

Mark R. Kramer, a senior lecturer at Harvard Business School and a cofounder and managing director of FSG, a global social-impact consulting firm, has weighed in on this merging of the public and private sectors. "We must stop pretending that business somehow exists in a vacuum that neither affects nor depends on the wellbeing of our society," Kramer wrote in the *Harvard Business Review* in 2019, citing "a growing body of evidence [that] demonstrates that economic success is strongly determined by the way a company addresses social issues." There is a competitive edge to be gained by those companies that recognize and celebrate the diversity of both consumers and employees, Kramer and his colleagues have learned in their research, good news for businesspeople wondering what's in it for them. "Committing to a purpose and having a positive social impact is increasingly central to good management and shareholder value," he concluded, Milton Friedman's socially blind thesis thankfully retired.[20]

That 40% of world commerce today is done by multinational corporations is yet more reason why social responsibility is in ascent. CSR functions as a kind of cultural Esperanto that people around the world can speak, magnifying both the positive and negative actions a company takes. Many organizations are gradually accepting and then embracing socially responsible efforts as the rationale for doing so becomes clearer. CSR "creates competitive advantages, positive brand I.D., crazy loyalty with employees, engages business partners, and electrifies corporate culture," stated Hannah Nokes, CEO of Magnify Impact, in 2019, citing numerous studies to back up those claims. In one study, two-thirds of consumers said they would pay more for a brand whose company has demonstrated some kind of social commitment, while another showed that 87% of consumers would buy a particular product if the company selling it supported an issue in which they believed.[21]

A Connected Economy

Like diversity and inclusion, social responsibility is being woven into various organizational departments, a clear sign that it is not a passing fad. "CSR has become the weapon of choice for what is known as, in corporate speak, the three R's: Investor Relations, Human Resources, and Public Relations," Sam Hill wrote for *Newsweek* in 2019, citing Starbuck's use of "ethically-sourced" coffee as a prime example of the newest version of social responsibility. "Sustainability" has become the most commonly spoken and heard buzzword in CSR circles, extending the use and meaning of the term from its environmentalist roots. In August of that year, almost two hundred CEOs of the nation's biggest companies signed a business roundtable statement committing to managing their organizations not just for shareholders but also for customers, employees, suppliers, and communities. Experts in the field maintain that CSR efforts are measurable, satisfying those concerned about the haziness of nice-sounding but less than quantifiable phrases like "doing well by doing good."[22]

ESG investors are particularly concerned that what Hill called "Do-Gooders Inc." translates into real numbers. Ratings are heavily relied upon by portfolio managers, both in terms of returns and how companies are performing per ESG metrics. Most investment firms have gotten into the area, knowing that many of their clients are interested in having their money not just generate additional revenue but make the world a better place. (Twenty-six percent of professionally managed assets in the United States had ESG mandates in 2018, up from 11% in 2012, according to Deloitte.)[23] BlackRock, the world's biggest investment firm which manages some $6.5 trillion, has shown interest, much in part to its CEO, Lawrence Fink. "As divisions continue to deepen, companies must demonstrate their commitment to the countries, regions, and communities where they operate, particularly on issues central to the world's future prosperity," Fink told the company's clients in 2018, a message that appears to be resonating with investors.[24]

It remains to be determined, however, whether BlackRock (and Goldman Sachs, which has also rhetorically committed to socially responsible investing) will significantly change the way they do business.[25] There are also some who believe that the largest investment firms are not interested in social responsibility for altruistic reasons but rather because it may represent the survival of their business. If the world's economy (or Earth itself) tanks, this thinking goes, the firms will have little or no money to invest for their clients (should there be any clients). "Firms that have trillions of dollars under management have no hedge against the global economy," Robert G. Eccles and Svetlana Klimenko wrote for the *Harvard Business Review* in 2019, suggesting that "they have become too big to let the planet fail." Climate change is indeed a big part of CSR, lending some weight to this theory.[26]

While Fink was for whatever reasons making ESG appear somewhat less woo-woo, he was following in the footsteps of economist Tim Nash who a decade earlier passionately advocated for responsible investing. Nash was at the time labeled a "tree hugger" but, now that Wall Street has boarded the train, it's clear that he was simply ahead of his time. Today, ESG is mostly about some aspect of environmentalism but employee diversity and inclusion, as well as community action, are often part of the equation. Millennials are said to be particularly attracted to ESG, part of their reputation as being the most socially conscious generation in history. (Seventy-seven percent of millennials are interested in social-impact investing and ownership, more than double the proportion of baby boomers, according to a Bloomberg Intelligence survey.)[27] Such investors want their financial strategy to be in sync with their moral and political beliefs and values, suggesting that ESG will grow exponentially in the years ahead as millennials become wealthier. It makes much sense that age friendliness be included in ESG rating criteria, either dovetailed into diversity and inclusion or as a separate initiative.[28]

Rocket Mortgage would likely score well on any ESG rating due to its extraordinary efforts to demonstrate social responsibility. In 2010, founder Dan Gilbert moved his company from Livonia, Michigan, to downtown Detroit (asking his thousands of employees, "Who's coming with me?!") The move by Rocket and its affiliated companies helped establish Detroit as the tech hub of the Midwest, this itself making a significant social and economic impact. It's through the company's "For More Than Profit" philosophy, however, that Rocket sets itself off from others treading the CSR waters. Team members (employees) are asked to make some kind of positive impact on the cities in which they live, mirroring the kind of activities that make up age-friendly communities. Hundreds of thousands of volunteer hours have been tallied in Detroit, this alongside the hundreds of millions of dollars in philanthropy and billions of dollars in development that the company has invested. Big Business should look to Rocket as a model to follow, especially by encouraging employees to contribute to the lives of local older citizens in some way.[29]

With regard to implementing CSR practices, however, Rocket is clearly more the exception than the rule. "Many companies care about corporate social responsibility," Christopher Wickert and Frank G.A. de Bakker wrote in the *Harvard Business Review* in 2019, "but putting it into practice requires more than CEO speeches and company policies." As with signing up to be an age-friendly company through AARP's LL&EL initiative, there is typically a big gap between top and middle management in terms of taking real action in CSR. Too often, middle managers see change as too difficult a process for them to take on, leaving things as business as usual. Based on their consulting work, Wickert and de Bakker outlined four tactics that could help turn social responsibility into real results rather than just politically correct words: (1) building a network of internal allies (teaming up with others to lead the charge), (2) making sustainability resonate (translating CSR from an abstract idea into daily routines), (3) identifying adequate incentives (making it clear why social responsibility matters), and (4) using external and internal benchmarking (measuring progress).[30]

When CSR is allowed to work, positive change usually follows. Having a strategy in place is increasingly recognized as a means to recruit and retain top talent, particularly among millennials and Gen Z. As well, according to Gallup, turnover has been shown to decrease when a company offers a skills-based volunteer program. Such a program allows employees to engage in some kind of community-based activity, making this a win-win initiative. More companies are making it possible for their workers to get involved in a local effort that, at the same time, enables the employees to learn a new skill. Getting out of the office and into the field is a great way to develop core talents, research demonstrates, a side benefit being the building of company loyalty.[31] Brooklyn-based Common Impact is one nonprofit that aligns businesses with social purpose with the goal of creating a "connected economy." "We envision a society in which all individuals and businesses invest their unique talents towards a shared purpose: strengthening the local communities in which we live and work," the organization states, CSR at its best.[32]

CSR can also contribute to what Bob Kelleher calls an "employment brand." Companies often know everything there is to know about their customers, using all kinds of research to parse their buying habits, but have little clue about their employees. Should it be any surprise that workers are often disengaged and ready to jump at another job opportunity? Kelleher asked in *Business NH Magazine.* (Leaders themselves often can't say why they worked at their companies.) Kelleher advised companies to develop an "employment brand" much like they have developed brands destined for the marketplace, using Timberland as an example. Timberland, best known for making and selling boots, understands the kind of people who are likely to succeed at the company, a big reason why it experiences low turnover and high profits. Timberland is also a purpose-driven company, with volunteerism a big part of what employees do when not producing very good boots. The case study suggests that creating socially responsible programs and policies—which include the presence of a multigenerational workforce—represents a powerful branding strategy for both consumers and employees.[33]

Growing With Age

As in the case of Timberland, offering employees volunteer benefits is an excellent way to achieve a "connected economy" and, more specifically, for Big Business to express age-friendly responsibility. Many companies in the United States, including Bank of America, Salesforce, Cisco, and Deloitte, offer such benefits, with some moving from a once-a-year campaign to an ongoing model. This kind of "prosocial" action allows companies to deepen relationships with local communities and increases employee engagement; the reason why they are sometimes called "corporate goodness" programs. With research showing that volunteer or pro bono programs often lead to higher productivity and lower turnover, it's not surprising that more companies are signing up. "Today's job seekers are looking for ways to find purpose in their work and align their personal values with their day-to-day jobs," Caitrin O'Sullivan, director of global communications for CSR at Prudential Financial, told *Employee Benefit News* in 2019. At Prudential, employees use their business expertise to assist nonprofit partners, an ideal matchmaking of corporate assets and social impact.[34]

Volunteer benefits take different forms at different companies. At Bank of America, employees can volunteer at an approved cause for up to two hours a week; in 2017, 200,000 employees around the world volunteered nearly two million hours. At Cisco, employees are allowed to take up to five days per year with pay to volunteer for a cause that is personally relevant. "By empowering our people to take time off to volunteer, we're collectively helping to change the world through active participation in our communities," says Francine Katsoudas, the company's chief people officer. At Deloitte, almost half of the company's 50,000 U.S. employees take part in Annual Impact Day, at which volunteers choose from 1 of about 1,000 project sites. TripAdvisor, meanwhile, sees volunteer benefits as part of the "employee experience," a nice way of integrating social responsibility into corporate identity.[35] And at Salesforce, employees are given seven days of volunteer time off to work with any nonprofit they choose, whether in this country or not. (Some have helped build homes in Cambodia, while others have helped local San Francisco kids learn about gardening.) Regardless of the specific cause, embedding the ethos of giving back in a company's culture is the key to effective CSR.[36]

While encouraging volunteerism enhances team morale, there are other ways for businesses to "pay it forward" and gain in the process. Allowing employees to do what they do well in a community setting helps build their skills and confidence, making them even better in the office. Organizing a team event serves as a reminder that a company is part of the larger community, something often overlooked by the split we create between public and private life. Sponsoring a charity event or fundraising walk to raise money for a local cause may be old school but still brings an organization closer together with community stakeholders. Finally, supporting small businesses is a means for big companies to bridge the social and economic divisions within a community, particularly as related to class.[37]

With good now the new cool within the world of business, it's an ideal time for Big Business to embrace age friendliness in any and all ways. Although aging is arguably the biggest story of our time and place, at least from a people perspective, it is conspicuously absent from the CSR conversation. Call it what you will—conscious capitalism, elevated economics, woke capitalism, sustainability, or greening—CSR and its sibling ESG have not acknowledged the major injustices routinely and consistently directed to older workers, consumers, and citizens.

Why is this so? Great strides have been made with regard to equal rights for women and people of color in the workplace and elsewhere, and many companies are now actively taking progressive steps to support the LGBTQ+ community. In 2021, for example, Alliant Energy, Franklin Templeton, and TIAA were each named by the Human Rights Campaign as a "Best Place to Work for LGBTQ+ Equality," designations that were proudly announced in the media. Is there a similar designation for "Best Place to Work for People 50 Years Old or Older"? If not, why? Don't older Americans deserve the same rights and protections afforded to other groups that have experienced discrimination? The message being sent by Corporate America is that the tens of millions of baby boomers are less deserving of full equality than others, a strange and disturbing thing.[38]

The material presented in this chapter would suggest that the stars are very nicely aligned for an age-friendly business climate. The social and governance dimensions of all-the-rage ESG, the eagerness for companies to be designated B Corporations, the purpose-driven strategies recommended by management consultants, and the rush toward diversity and inclusion would seem to propel the social and economic implications of an aging population. This has not been the case, leading one to conclude that ageism is directly responsible. Companies will pay the closest attention to environmental concerns—whether, say, the cups used in the cafeteria are not just recyclable but locally sourced and made with 100% organic materials—but screen out older applicants for jobs they are well qualified to fill. This has to change and soon, as boomers aren't getting younger.

One of the more peculiar things about the private sector's snubbing of older people is the public sector's embrace of these same folks. As Chapter 2 showed in considerable detail, small towns and big cities in this country and elsewhere are avidly seeking WHO's and AARP's designation as an age-friendly community, with civic leaders fully aware of the challenges and opportunities that an aging population represents. Communities are expending much effort and significant resources to redesign and improve their built environments and broaden their portfolio of services, a massive undertaking that is costing billions of dollars and innumerable person hours.

Big Business, meanwhile, is making virtually no effort to extend such a welcome to older people; in fact, it is making a concerted effort to exclude them as workers, consumers, and citizens, seeing little or no value in making them part of their respective organization's mission and everyday practices. How could one group of people see things so differently from another group of people, even when some of them are the same people? Some of those taking part in age-friendly community programs no doubt work for local companies that are pursuing age-unfriendly policies, in other words, making this paradox yet more incomprehensible. An HR manager helping rake the leaves on the front lawn of a senior citizen may the very next day toss out the resume of an older job applicant because of his or her age, a truly schizophrenic scenario. Building in a work component into AARP's Age-Friendly Communities program represents a huge opportunity to address the strange contradiction of older people being welcome in all kinds of public settings but not in the workplace.

Thankfully, some steps are being taken to try to bring some measure of sense and sensibility to what is one of our worst social problems. In a separate initiative, AARP is taking a leadership role in advocating for the legal rights of older Americans, especially as related to work. In 2021, for example, AARP along with the AARP Foundation and the National Employment Lawyers Association urged the United States Court of Appeals for the Sixth Circuit to reverse an appeals court ruling in an age discrimination lawsuit. The case involved a former

Ohio bank teller who was fired from her job at age 47. The court ruled that the woman had to prove that her age was the "sole cause" of her termination, an absurd mandate given all the variables in play and potential reasons an employer can conjure up. "Placing the burden on older workers to show age discrimination as the sole cause of an adverse employment decision would make it nearly impossible to prove illegal bias based on age," stated AARP Foundation senior vice president for litigation William Alvarado Rivera, making the much more basic argument that "age should play no role in any employment decision." The decision—the latest of a long line of failures by the justice system in the area of age discrimination—had far-reaching implications for potentially millions of older workers.[39]

Ironically, AARP had just launched a new digital platform called "Growing with Age" designed to illustrate the benefits that companies could realize through a multigenerational workforce. The interactive platform made available tools, research, and resources for employers, building on AARP's successful LL&EL initiative. Astutely, AARP positioned "Growing with Age" as a logical extension of diversity and inclusion, leveraging a finding from a recent survey of 6,000 employers in 36 countries. Eighty-three percent of global business leaders recognized that multigenerational workforces are key to the growth and long-term success of their companies, according to the survey, but most employers had yet to include age as a factor in their company's diversity and inclusion policies.[40]

Long Overdue

AARP's "Growing with Age" platform also built on findings from a recently published issue brief titled "Global Insights on the Multigenerational Workforce." Not surprisingly, the brief made the well-documented case that older workers are staying in the workforce longer and playing significant roles in organizations but often face workplace discrimination because of their age. Older workers don't receive the same level of training as younger workers, something that not only puts them at a career disadvantage but also reinforces ageist stereotypes. More enlightened people in the human resources field recognize that problem, however, and advise colleagues to avoid it. "Too many companies fall short of embracing older workers' needs," wrote I. Shaun Gholston in *Talent Development* in 2020, thinking that employers themselves needed some training in terms of benefiting from an age-diverse workforce. "Craft an age-diverse and inclusive talent strategy that develops all employees' critical digital and cognitive capabilities, social and emotional skills, and adaptability and resilience," Gholston told readers, an approach that would ultimately improve companies' bottom-lines.[41]

The decision by Corporate America to not include age as part of a diversity and inclusion initiative is all the more inane in that there is much evidence to show that age bias is costing companies and the United States billions of dollars each year. Older workers (age 50 and up) would have contributed $850 billion more in 2018 to the GDP if they could have remained in or reentered the labor force, switched jobs, or been promoted internally, research by AARP and the Economist Intelligence Unit showed. It appeared that the usual myths—that older workers cost too much and are technologically illiterate—were largely responsible for the bias, overpowering the actual truths—that they are highly dependable, can often solve problems that younger people cannot, and don't get rattled if or when a crisis appears.[42]

Catherine Collinson, CEO and president of the nonprofit Transamerica Institute and its Transamerica Center for Retirement Studies®, is one of the country's loudest voices calling for a multigenerational workforce. "Today's environment requires unprecedented levels of innovation, problem solving, agility and adaptability," she wrote in *Benefits Quarterly* in 2021, thinking that the knowledge, skills, and experiences to be found within a multigenerational workforce was a good foundation for high-performing teams. As well, issues were addressed more efficiently and effectively when team members were of different ages, much like that regarding gender and race. "Age-friendly employers embody an inclusive, diverse and multigenerational workforce," she reiterated, with research showing that such employers "foster an environment in which workers of all ages can fully contribute and succeed."[43]

In its 2020 research, LinkedIn, the world's largest professional network, also found that ageism in the workplace was doing serious damage to the global economy and to individuals' lives. About 45% of baby boomers said in a survey that they did not have the financial resources to pursue their personal passions because of their status as older workers, with roughly the same percentage concerned that joblessness would lead to inactive bodies and minds. The findings indicated that a multigenerational workforce was the logical solution. "This calls for businesses to recognize that the different age groups can complement and help one another," LinkedIn concluded, thinking much like Collinson that "more companies can be an enabler of change and foster an inclusive workforce to help everyone succeed."[44]

If such voices of reason cannot change the ways of Big Business, perhaps the legal system can. Just as many lawmakers are seeking to make their respective states age friendly, so are they introducing legislation to end age discrimination in the workplace. In Connecticut in 2021, for example, state Senator Derek Slap (D-West Hartford) championed the drafting of a bill that would protect older workers from discrimination; the bill was unanimously approved by the legislature's Aging Committee (of which Slap was chair). Senate Bill 56, "An Act

Deterring Age Discrimination in Employment Application," prohibited employers from asking for date of birth and school graduation and/or attendance dates on job applications. (The bill would allow for prospective employers to ask about a date of birth if there is a bona fide occupational need or if state or federal laws require it.) If enacted, Connecticut will be one of just a few states that explicitly bans this information from job applications. "No one should be vetted for a job because of their age, and this bill closes a costly loophole for older workers," Slap said, something the country's courts might want to consider in their rulings.[45] Slap went further than just introducing the bill by extending the opportunity for state residents to offer their personal testimony on the issue (via Zoom), allowing legislators to hear real stories of age discrimination in the workplace.[46]

Lawmakers in New Jersey, too, are responding to their constituents' demand for age equality in the workplace. Within days of the action in Connecticut, the New Jersey Assembly's Aging and Senior Services Committee advanced legislation sponsored by Assembly Democrats Valerie Vainieri Huttle and Angela McKnight. Bill A-681 was comprehensive in scope. If passed, it would prohibit governmental employers from requiring retirement at a certain age, bar employers from refusing to hire someone for the sole reason that they are over 70 years old, lift limitations on employees seeking claims of unlawfully being required to retire, and prohibit higher education institutions from requiring tenured employees to retire at age 70. Like most states (and the country as a whole), New Jersey had laws on its books that permitted discrimination, something Bill A-681 was specifically designed to address. "This legislation is long overdue," Huttle and McKnight said, adding that "It's time to update our State laws to fully prohibit age discrimination in the workplace and open doors for older workers to stay employed."[47]

Things are cooking at the federal level as well in terms of making the American workplace more inclusive through legislation. In 2021, Representative Suzanne Bonamici (D-Oregon) was unanimously reelected to chair the Subcommittee on Civil Rights and Human Services, leading legislation addressing civil rights, equal employment opportunities, human services, programs for seniors, and more. The congresswoman continued to serve as a member of the Subcommittee on Higher Education and Workforce Investment, where she also had shown deep concern for the well-being of older Americans. "Our workforce is becoming increasingly diverse, and yet too many women, people of color, older workers, workers with disabilities, and LGBTQ workers still experience harassment and discrimination in the workplace," Bonamici announced when reelected as subcommittee chair. Her efforts offered some hope that the federal government would view age much like race, gender, ability, and sexual orientation, and extend an equivalent level of legal protections.[48] Representative Steve Cohen (D-TN) has also consistently supported rights for older workers in congressional voting, one reason why he received a 100% score from the Leadership Conference on Civil and Human Rights in 2020.[49]

While such state and federal attempts to bar age discrimination in the workplace was indeed long overdue, the challenge was perhaps even greater than these forward-thinking elected officials realized. For some time now, HR departments in many companies have used AI tools and platforms in their hiring practices that are designed to sort through job candidates and pick out the "best" ones based on assigned criteria. The problem is that the programs were almost certainly written by white males in their 20s and 30s, embedding biases based on race, gender, and age into the process. Automation can be just as prejudiced as people, it turns out, a function of the language in the code used by the programmers. The resumes of women, people of color, and older workers can be instantly zapped out by AI systems, obviously a discriminatory practice that may also be eliminating some of the best candidates for the position. Tossing the technology in the dustbin would be the ideal solution but an unlikely one since companies believe the systems save them money and time. Using a diverse programming team to write the code seems to be the only viable means of eliminating the biases, but is the tech industry really going to hire 50- and 60-somethings to do that? (Indeed, such candidates for those programming jobs would be screened out by the technology!)[50]

A Rising Wave

With ageism a pervasive force not just in humans but also built into the technology used by Corporate America, it's clear that ending age discrimination in the workplace is a mighty challenge. While more brainy folks from the worlds of business and politics are certainly helping the cause, much of the responsibility falls on workers themselves, as it is they who bear the burden of the problem. Whether currently employed or unemployed, baby boomers represent a huge and powerful coalition who wield tremendous economic and political clout. As consumers, older Americans can sway marketers to do the right thing and be age friendly in all of their business operations, including hiring and firing. Given their activist roots, boomers can and should take on ageism as a battle to be fought much like they combated the injustices of the Vietnam War, racism, and gender discrimination a half-century ago. There is now a renaissance of social activism, and baby boomers now have the opportunity to create real and positive change. Doing so will add to their already proud legacy.

What Forrest Briscoe and Abhinav Gupta called "business disruption from the inside out" is another tool in older workers' toolbox. Writing in *Stanford Social Innovation Review* in 2021, Briscoe and Gupta documented the rather startling degree of employee activism that has recently taken place in this country. Thousands of workers at different companies including Amazon, Google, Facebook, and even Disney have publicly protested a decision made by management, hearkening back to the strikes by workers decades ago in pursuit of higher wages or improved benefits. There is "a rising wave of employee activism—when employees advocate for social change inside, and sometimes even criticize, their own organization," the two observed, thinking that "this trend has had a range of consequences for both employees and the workplace." CSR has often been the focus of employee activism, the latter seen as a means to encourage management to put more consciousness into capitalism. According to Briscoe and Gupta, four macro trends have accounted for the spike in employee activism: rising workforce expectations, empowerment as a management principle, urgent societal challenges, and new technologies.[51]

So how could older workers make their voices heard to end age discrimination in the workplace? First, analyze the conditions, Briscoe and Gupta recommend, meaning find the right time and place for action. Unemployed workers have little or nothing to lose, after all, but management may retaliate against current activist employers (Google did just that). Framing the issue also helps (such as by contextualizing ageism within diversity and inclusion), as does utilizing knowledge of the organization (does the company have a history of ageist practices?) and leveraging networks (can AARP or another organization be of help?). "Employee activists are part of an increasingly complex stakeholder landscape that business leaders face today," the authors concluded, good news for the millions of older workers fighting for equal rights.[52]

Not just workers but also investors can help shape corporate policies with regard to age. As the growth of ESG suggests, more investors are putting their money where their mouths are, making companies pay more attention to social responsibility. In *Crain's Chicago Business* in 2021, Judith Crown called this form of impact investing "Capitalism 2.0," an appraisal of not just the size of profits but also how they are generated. With ESG increasingly top of mind in the financial sphere, in other words, we have the opportunity to make age friendliness part of the criteria used by asset managers in developing their portfolios and funds. Determining an organization's "age-positive" (or "age-negative") score is a way for both asset managers and individuals to decide if a publicly traded company warrants investment dollars, a powerful incentive to make positive change. Such a score would be based on the hiring and retention of older employees, as well as other age-based practices. Seen within the context of diversity and inclusion initiatives or, more broadly, sustainability, "age investing" is not as farfetched as one might think, especially given the collective economic power of baby boomers.[53]

Legal action, or even the threat of such, should be considered a last resort when an older person faces discrimination based on age in the workplace. Such situations are expensive, stressful, and time-consuming, especially when there's a contentious relationship between the two sides. (Companies also usually have a lot more money and access to lawyers than individuals.) As well, while the ADEA has no doubt discouraged some employers from firing or demoting an employee considered past his or her prime or deemed too costly, the courts have made it difficult for plaintiffs to win their cases. Still, 15,573 charges were filed with the Equal Employment Opportunity Commission alleging age discrimination in 2019, which was about 21% of all cases filed. It's in the best interests of companies to avoid being charged with such, of course, not just because of the expense involved but also the risk of reputational damage. With the current pressure for companies to be good guys higher than ever, it makes no sense for any company to engage in unlawful employment practices of any kind, including those related to age.[54]

An even more compelling reason for companies to avoid age-based discrimination includes the benefits to be gained through a multigeneration workforce. Thomas Scroggins, a Birmingham, Alabama-based attorney who has experience in these matters, has offered good advice to managers not wanting to find themselves in a courtroom or writing a fat check to a disgruntled employee. The first step is to set and communicate policies regarding discrimination of any kind; most workers understand the rules regarding race and gender but simply don't realize that they apply to older people as well. Next, leaders have to set a good example by not just talking the talk but walking the walk, i.e., acting as a champion for anti-ageism. Dropping the stereotypes is another of Scroggins's tips, meaning not assuming that an older employee can't perform a particular task because of his or her age. As well, as Gholston advised, training and development opportunities should be for everyone—not just younger employees—and teams should consist of people of different ages, just as one wouldn't intentionally form a team solely based on race or gender. "Recognizing the value of a multigenerational workforce is not a challenge," Scroggins wrote in *BenefitsPRO* in 2020, but rather "an opportunity to develop an agile workforce and a competitive edge."[55]

An Age-Neutral Workplace

Businesses of all shapes and sizes can benefit greatly by taking such a view. In their article "The AGE Model: Addressing Ageism in the Workplace Through Corporate Social Responsibility" published in the *Journal of Labor and Society* in 2019, Virginia Cortijo, Lee Phillip Mcginnis, and Elif Sisli-Ciamarra explained how the challenges associated with aging populations are too complex for governments to solve alone. "Companies can play a significant role in combating the economic and social costs of an aging society through their Corporate Social Responsibility practices," the three wrote, suggesting that businesses consider something they called an "Acknowledge-Grow-Embrace (AGE)" framework as a practical model. In order to take advantage of the diversity of thought, experiences, and skills of an age-diverse workforce and create one that is sustainable and socially responsible, the authors argued, companies should (1) acknowledge that an organization may be practicing or allowing ageism activities and structures to persist in the firm, (2) grow an understanding of the different forms and levels of ageism present in their companies, and (3) embrace employees of all ages and encourage them to share their knowledge and leverage their potential.[56]

While such a model is largely alien to Big Businesses, some rather under-the-radar organizations have shown they fully appreciate the value of an age-friendly workforce. One outfit that clearly gets it is the Army Sustainment Command (ASC), which is the logistics arm of the Army Materiel Command that is charged with providing soldiers with everything they need to do their jobs, i.e., ammunition, equipment, food, uniforms, and much more. With about a thousand employees at its headquarters at Rock Island, Illinois (some military but mostly civilians), and another 40,000 scattered around the world, the ASC is a very large and diverse organization.[57]

One might not think that any part of the U.S. Army would be more progressive about inclusiveness than say, Google or Facebook, but that is precisely the case. Just like a major corporation, the ASC has to recruit and retain good employees, but the military organization is different in that it fully appreciates age diversity. The age of ASC employees ranges from their early 20s to their late 80s, quite a mix of Gen Z, millennials, Gen X, baby boomers, and members of the Silent Generation. The influx of younger workers into the mix as older workers retire or die and take their knowledge with them is a challenge that the ASC has met through an intensive mentoring program. Likewise, through "reverse mentoring," younger workers share their more technical knowledge with older ones, an exchange that helps to bridge generational divides. "Ideally, we leverage the significant amount of experience and wisdom in the seasoned force to mentor and develop the junior workers as part of a sustainable succession plan," explained Dan Kern, ASC's Civilian Personnel Division chief, in 2021, echoing Chip Conley's vision of elderhood in the workplace.[58]

The ASC's view of age diversity is something that Silicon Valley's best and brightest can learn much from. The Army unit is trying to achieve what Kern calls an "age-neutral workplace," a very nice way of framing how long employees have happened to live. "If we look at diversity and inclusion from the lens of the gifts that each individual brings to the team without passing perceptions of that individual through the filters of generational expectations," he added, "we are truly meeting the intent of a strong diversity and inclusion program."[59]

Well said, indeed, but Debra Born, writing for triplepundit.com in 2020, deserves the final words on the subject. "Older employees feel unwelcome in Corporate America," Born plainly put it, thinking that many of them have been "left behind." Much to the surprise of economists who had predicted baby boomers would retire in their 60s, much like the latter's parents, most members of this generation have chosen to remain in the workforce. Employers, despite their rhetorical commitment to be socially responsible organizations, seem equally taken aback, not prepared to adapt to the reality of a multigenerational workforce. Too often those in their 50s, 60s, and 70s are viewed as workers of the past and relics of a different age. Even those in their 40s are not infrequently facing age discrimination, AARP's research shows, and anyone over 35 is labeled a "dinosaur" in the tech industry. The cost of older workers, especially with regard to health care, is usually blamed as the primary culprit, but there is no doubt that culturally rooted ageism is playing a major role in experienced employees getting left behind. (Only 8% of companies include age in their diversity and inclusion initiatives, according to a 2019 study by PwC.) "Sexism and racism are hot topics in the news every day, but ageism is a growing diversity and inclusion issue that continues to be swept under the rug," Born wrote, adding that "these workers, along with their families, are suffering as a result."[60]

With 85% of boomers planning to work, if possible, into their 70s and even 80s, according to AARP, older workers represent not just the past but also the future. The number of people aged 65 and older will increase from 48 million to 88 million by 2050, according to the U.S. Census Bureau, a statistic that should incentivize companies to not only keep them around but hire more of them. Rather than push them out the door, in other words, Big Business should recognize older workers as valuable resources who will continue to contribute to a company's success, however measured. AARP's research has demonstrated the wide range of qualities and skills that any organization seeks in its employees, such as loyalty, productivity, motivation, the ability to work under pressure, leadership, problem-solving, commitment to their work, and, of course, experience. "Instead of sending them away, employers would be wise to welcome and appreciate older workers as the 'valued resource' they are," Born concluded, suggesting that truly age-friendly organizations should "let the days of [their] watching sunsets on the porch wait."[61]

Notes

1 "Greed Is Good. Except When It's Bad," *New York Times Magazine*, September 13, 2020.

2 "Greed Is Good. Except When It's Bad."

3 Derrick Feldmann and Michael Alberg-Seberich, *The Corporate Social Mind: How Companies Lead Social Change from the Inside Out* (New York: Fast Company Press, 2020) 1–6.

4 Richard Steel, *Elevated Economics: How Conscious Consumers Will Fuel the Future of Business* (New York: Fast Company Press, 2020).

5 Deborah Capras, "A Higher Purpose," *Business Spotlight*, April 2020, 28–29.

6 Witold Henisz, Tim Koller, and Robin Nuttall, "Five Ways That ESG Creates Value," *McKinsey Quarterly*, 2019.

7 Stephanie Mehta, "A Better Way of Doing Business," *Fast Company*, October/November 2020.

8 Indra K. Nooyi and Vijay Govindarajan, "Becoming a Better Corporate Citizen," *Harvard Business Review*, March/April 2020.

9 Kristin Toussaint, "Beyond Woke Capitalism," *Fast Company*, October/November 2020.

10 Keith Mestrich, Mark A. Pinsky, Lindsay Blakely, and Bill Saporito "The Rise and Rise of Business as a Force for Good," *Inc.*, November 2019.

11 Hank Gilman, "Companies Are Digging Deeper," *Newsweek Global*, July 10, 2020.

12 Paul Polman, Raj Sisodia, and Kip Tindell, "What Good Business Looks Like," *Harvard Business Review*, May 13, 2020, 1–4.

13 Jinglian Wu, "Shifting to a Stakeholder Economy," *Stanford Social Innovation Review*, Spring 2019.

14 Justin Dawes, "Business, Charitable Sectors Are Blurring," *Grand Rapids Business Journal*, March 8, 2019.

15 Erika Bolstad, "Good Is the New Green," *Oregon Business Magazine*, June 2019.

16 Max H. Bazerman, "A New Model for Ethical Leadership," *Harvard Business Review*, September/October 2020.

17 O.K. Carter, "Millennials and Gen X-ers Are Expected to Significantly Change the Concept of Corporate Social Responsibility," *Fort Worth Business Press*, December 16, 2019, 10.

18 "Millennials and Gen X-ers Are Expected to Significantly Change the Concept of Corporate Social Responsibility."

19 Alana Semuels, "Values Added," *Time International*, December 2, 2019.

20 Mark R. Kramer, "The Backlash to Larry Fink's Letter Shows How Far Business Has to Go on Social Responsibility," *Harvard Business Review*, January 31, 2019, 3.

21 "Millennials and Gen X-ers Are Expected to Significantly Change the Concept of Corporate Social Responsibility."

22 Sam Hill, "Do-Gooders Inc.," *Newsweek Global*, December 6, 2019.

23 Peter Coy, "Is It All About Money?" *Bloomberg Businessweek*, December 28, 2020.

24 "Do-Gooders Inc."

25 Amy Cortese, "Banking for Good," *Crain's New York Business*, January 7, 2019.

26 Robert G. Eccles and Svetlana Klimenko, "The Investor Revolution," *Harvard Business Review*, May–June 2019, 110.

27 Chris Stokel-Walker, "MBA Recruiters Rank Candidates' ESG Experience Dead Last," *Bloomberg.com*, March 18, 2020.

28 Brenda Bouw, "Making Money Work for You—and the Planet," *Maclean's*, March 2020.

29 Dan Gilbert, "Inside Rocket Mortgage's 'For More Than Profit' Philosophy," *Forbes*, December 2020.

30 Christopher Wickert and Frank G.A. de Bakker, "How CSR Managers Can Inspire Other Leaders to Act on Sustainability, "*Harvard Business Review*, January 10, 2019, 2–5.

31 Danielle Holly, "Attract and Retain Talent With CSR Programs," *TD: Talent Development*, April 2019, 102–103.

32 commonimpact.org.

33 Bob Kelleher, "What Is Your Employment Brand?" *BusinessNHmagazine.com*, May 2019, 8.

34 Amanda Schiavo and Caroline Hroncich, "Seeing Value in Volunteer Benefits," *Employee Benefit News*, July/August 2019, 24–25.

35 Kathryn Mayer, "7 Employers with Top Volunteer Benefits," *Employee Benefit News*, July/August 2019, 24–25.

36 Richard Jerome and Hanna Flanagan, "50 Companies That Care," *People*, August 5, 2019, 75.

37 Katie Zwetzig, "5 Ways to Pay It Forward," *TD: Talent Development*, July 2019, 72.

38 "Alliant Energy Named a 'Best Place to Work for LGBTQ+ Equality,'" *Targeted News Service*, January 29, 2021; "Franklin Templeton Receives Top Marks in 2021 Corporate Equality Index," *Targeted News Service*, January 28, 2021; "TIAA Earns 'Best Places to Work for LGBTQ Equality' Designation," *Targeted News Service*, February 3, 2021.

39 "AARP, AARP Foundation and NELA Urge U.S. Court of Appeals to Reverse 'Sole Cause' Decision That Threatens Older Workers," *Targeted News Service*, February 2021.

40 "AARP Launches New Digital Platform, 'Growing With Age,' to Help Businesses Reap Benefits of Multigenerational Workforces," *Targeted News Service*, December 17, 2020.

41 I. Shaun Gholston, "Train Employers to Lead an Age-Diverse Workforce," *Talent Development*, November 2020, 14–15.

42 Anonymous, "Age Bias Costs U.S. Economy $850B," *Journal of Business* (Spokane, Washington), February 13, 2020, 20, 23.

43 Catherine Collinson, "Amid the Pandemic: Seven Win-Win Solutions to Support Employee Health and Financial Well-Being," *Benefits Quarterly*, First Quarter 2021, 16.

44 "Age Is a Key Barrier to Work Opportunities for People: LinkedIn Opportunity Index," *Targeted News Service*, February 12, 2020.

45 "Aging Committee Takes Aim at Age Discrimination," *US Fed News Service, Including US State News*, January 19, 2021.

46 "Sen. Slap Encourages Public to Testify on Bill Opposing Age Discrimination in the Hiring Process," *US Fed News Service, Including US State News*, February 4, 2021.

47 "Assembly Democrats Vainieri Huttle and McKnight Bill to Expand Law Prohibiting Age Discrimination Passes Committee," *US Fed News Service, Including US State News*, January 14, 2021.

48 "Rep. Bonamici to Lead Education and Labor Subcommittee on Civil Rights and Human Services," *Targeted News Service*, February 9, 2021.

49 "Rep. Cohen Receives 100% Score From Leadership Conference on Civil, Human Rights," *Targeted News Service*, November 3, 2020.

50 Dan Cook, "Banishing Bias in the Workplace—and in Benefits," *BenefitsPRO*, July 16, 2019.

51 Forrest Briscoe and Abhinav Gupta, "Business Disruption from the Inside Out," *Stanford Social Innovation Review*, Winter 2021, 48–54.

52 "Business Disruption from the Inside Out."

53 Judith Crown, "Capitalism 2.0: Socially Conscious Investing Gains Currency as Investors Seek to Improve Sustainability and Benefit the Social Good While Still Making Money," *Crain's Chicago Business*, February 22, 2021, 15.

54 Thomas Scroggins, "Capitalizing on Your Multi-generational Workforce," *BenefitsPRO*, Apr 17, 2020.

55 "Capitalizing on Your Multi-generational Workforce."

56 Virginia Cortijo, Lee Phillip Mcginnis, and Elif Sisli-Ciamarra, "The AGE Model: Addressing Ageism in the Workplace Through Corporate Social Responsibility," *Journal of Labor and Society*, January 2019.

57 "Project Inclusion: Treating Employees as Unique Individuals Best Way for Army Sustainment Command to Retain, Recruit Workforce," *Targeted News Service*, January 26, 2021.

58 "Project Inclusion: Treating Employees as Unique Individuals Best Way for Army Sustainment Command to Retain, Recruit Workforce."

59 "Project Inclusion: Treating Employees as Unique Individuals Best Way for Army Sustainment Command to Retain, Recruit Workforce."

60 Debra Born, "Left Behind: Older Employees Feel Unwelcome in Corporate America," *triplepundit.com*, January 17, 2020.

61 "Left Behind: Older Employees Feel Unwelcome in Corporate America."

Chapter 6

Conclusion

The Rolling Stones, who began this story, have no intention of watching sunsets on the porch, at least of this writing. With an average age of about 75, the bandmates are more in line with what Bradley Schurman calls the "super age," the emerging world in which people live, work, and enjoy longer, sometimes dramatically longer lives. But like the Stones, many biologically older people are rejecting the traditional narrative of aging and are doing what they've done for decades or starting something entirely new. In fact, I find the Rolling Stones and most septuagenarians way cooler than when they were young. Their bodies have changed, of course, but they seem wiser and happier people, a fair exchange, I think.

Unfortunately, society hasn't quite caught up with the people. American culture is still listening to big band music, metaphorically speaking, not at all in touch with the ways that older people are living their lives. Myths and stereotypes rooted in mid-20th-century thinking are pervasive, stronger in fact than the realities that we can actually see and hear. Ageism certainly isn't America at its best, I hope we can agree, and not at all what this country is supposed to be about. In fact, I'd say it's at our worst, a direct contradiction to the ethos of equality that the Founding Fathers brilliantly conceived two-and-a-half centuries ago. (An aside: the average age of the signers of the Declaration of Independence was 44, making it unlikely that any of them would get hired by a big company today for a managerial position.)

Ageism is particularly disturbing given the fact that all of us are aging all the time, and it is only the lucky ones who make it to old age. While aging is a universal experience, younger people (and some older ones, interestingly) view those with more years in their life as the "other," a means of identifying who one is and isn't. Through ageism, we can vent our fears of dependence and death onto others, making it their problem and not ours. Older people are a convenient target of the anxiety and insecurity we feel about what is the ultimate existential dilemma of life: that it is certain to end. We blame old people for this troublesome truth, projecting onto them an inner angst that each of us carries around all the time at a greater or lesser level. We objectify older people, a way to safely contain the unsolvable problem that one day we too will disappear.[1]

When will we move from the denial and anger associated with aging to acceptance? Why can't we fully humanize older people and treat them as equals? Ageism today is a powerful combination of the minor occurrences found in everyday life and the major discriminations expressed by Corporate America and the legal system. The two varieties reinforce each other, creating a potent synergy that can make the situation seem hopeless. Anti-agers feed on this hatred of oldness, teasing us with the seductiveness of youthful beauty and, in a sense, immortality. Needless to say, this is a tough hand to beat, as the cards appear stacked against the possibility of ever turning our negative view of aging into a positive one.

Given how entrenched ageism is in American society, it would be easy to conclude that ending it is an unachievable goal. Indeed, based on the abundance of evidence, one could fairly say that the United States really is no country for old men (and women) and that creating a truly age friendly nation is a long shot at best. While the age friendly movement continues to grow (the March 2021 United Nations Global Report on Ageism was an especially welcome development), I believe that much of the conversation to date has been preaching to the choir, meaning significant impact has not been made outside the relatively small circle of people who are already convinced that changing the narrative of aging should be a priority. Beyond all the data, personal experience tells me this is so. I sometimes apply for jobs that I am well qualified for as a kind of anthropological field test of ageism. I am never granted an interview much less an offer, even with a company that bought a company I happen to have founded a couple of decades ago. In fact, I cannot get an entry-level position with this company solely because of my age, a fair reflection of how deeply embedded the ethos of ageism is in Big Business today.

With such personal experience, and similar stories I hear from many other sexagenarians facing job discrimination, it's not surprising that I have designated Corporate America as primarily responsible for the ageism that exists today in the United States. For better or worse, the economy is the backbone of our society, and the management of major companies should be nothing less than ashamed by their treatment of older adults, both as workers and consumers. These people (and it's important to remember that it is people, not organizations, who are ultimately responsible for any and all actions taken and not taken) wield enormous power, and they have abused it by actively treating people of age (or "agers," as some are now referring to older people) unfairly. Over half of American adults are 45 years old or older, making me wonder what percentage of new hires fall into this demographic. As well, research has shown that the presence of an age friendly workplace would create a positive ripple effect throughout society in terms of ending ageism, even more reason why Big Business should demonstrate its rhetorical commitment to both diversity and inclusion and social responsibility.

History, however, tells another story. Few Americans a hundred years ago could predict that an African American would become president of the United States and a female African American would become vice president, proof that the future is unpredictable, especially regarding social change. If we can radically transform our view of race and gender, can't we do the same for aging, especially given that it happens to all of us? The circumstances surrounding age are very different from those of race and gender, of course, but make no mistake— ageism is a civil rights issue. It may take a generation or two or three, but our past suggests that our future may be a very different one regarding our view of how long a person has been alive.

To that point, much like the feminist and civil rights movements, which each began with a grassroots form of activism, there are today many signs of a burgeoning aging movement. Thousands of people have enlisted in the cause in some way, making their voices heard in whatever way they can. And unlike trailblazers of the past seeking equality, we have websites, blogs, email, and social media, exponentially extending the ability to connect with others and share our thoughts in real time. In addition to this bottom-up approach, organizations of considerable size and with substantial resources are exerting a top-down effort to change the narrative of aging.

The United Nations (UN) is also taking steps to propel an age-friendly movement via a proposed Convention on the Rights of Older Persons. The treaty, which is likely to be the next major human rights treaty adopted by the UN, will seek to reaffirm critical human rights for older people around the world. As AARP's partnerships with WHO, the OECD, and WEF demonstrate, more global alliances are being formed as any and all practices of ageism are further exposed as unethical and ultimately unsustainable. With the world watching, there is a chance that much progress can be made over the next couple of decades as the silver tsunami crashes on our demographic shores.

The prospect of true age equality or neutrality represents a huge cultural shift, so there's no doubt it will take time to happen. We are still dealing with racism and gender discrimination, of course, so the process would be a gradual one. Our best hope may be with Generation Z or Alpha (those born in the early 2010s), as those groups are very ethnically and racially diverse and may perceive age as just one more biological trait. Differences of any kind will be increasingly accepted in the decades ahead of us, I believe, a reason to be optimistic about where we are headed. Age may very well be accommodated within this broader interpretation of pluralism, getting us closer to our motto of "out of many, one." Groups now considered the minority will become the majority of the nation's population around 2045, according to the Census, so that may indeed serve as a tipping point of sorts in terms of how older Americans are treated as workers, consumers, and citizens.

Much like racism and gender discrimination, however, it is unlikely that ageism will just magically disappear, so it is up to us to fight against it. Cultural biases are often handed down from one generation to another, making it imperative that we let younger people know that oppression directed against any group of people based on their physical attributes is unacceptable. Negative perceptions about age start very young, so we should instill the concept of age friendliness in children much like how anti-racism is taught in schools every day in this country (often through a lens of history).

All forms of social activism are difficult, it needs to be said, as they inherently create conflict, tension, and unease. AARP uses the term "disrupt" to describe what needs to happen to the narrative of aging, making it clear that our apple cart has to be upset if we are to realize fairness and equality. But activism is in this country's DNA, of course, making the pursuit of age friendliness entirely consistent with our determination to call attention to conditions that are morally unjust with the goal of correcting them. We have a responsibility to live up to our nation's ideals and our long history of fighting for what we believe in. We're not a content people; our values are rooted in progress and moving forward, and we've shown over and over that we're not afraid of challenging the status quo. We need to demonstrate this same kind of commitment to defeating ageism so that we can take one more step toward achieving the society of which we are capable.

The flourishing of age-friendly communities across the country and world shows that despite the many obstacles this can be done. Incentivized by both civic responsibility and economic considerations, communities of all stripes are eagerly courting older residents and exerting great effort to attract and retain them. A healthy community is a diverse one, local leaders understand, making a multigenerational population a much-sought-after goal. Small towns and big cities are thinking globally and acting locally—the heart and soul of the age-friendly proposition. Rather than just talk about inclusiveness, communities are demonstrating it in many different ways, even if it means tearing up sidewalks or spending money for more benches in the public parks. This is America at its best, doing what it takes to make life better for all the people. Even if they are heavily financially motivated—older people who can afford it like to eat out a lot, keep some of their savings in banks that can be then loaned out, and spend absurd amounts of money on their children and grandchildren—age-friendly communities serve as hard evidence that older people do not have to be treated with scorn and derision.

If the mayor of a town with a smaller population than the number of employees of a Fortune 1000 corporation gets this, why can't Big Business? Why can't managers within Corporate America, especially those in HR, apply the successful model of age communities to the way they run their organizations? Businesspeople talk a lot about diversity and inclusion but are simply not interested in it regarding age and have admitted so. Less than 10% of D&I initiatives address ageism in the workplace, one survey showed, making the actual number likely even smaller. The truth is, although HR people will never say so because it is both unethical and illegal, that companies don't want older employees around, regardless of their race or gender (the bosses being the only exception). The fact that the people we have put in charge of diversity and inclusion are not really committed to diversity and inclusion is nothing less than tragic and serves as prime evidence of the degree to which older people are disliked in our society.

The irony involved is that companies have to go to far less trouble and expense than communities in becoming age friendly. Millions of dollars are typically spent to redevelop the built environment of a town or city, a huge strain on any budget. As well, all kinds of services are often added, these too involving great expense and a wholesale rethinking of what makes a community good for all its residents. Big Business has to resort to none of these drastic measures; rather, it just needs to be open to the idea of making workforces more multigenerational, mirroring life outside the company doors. No zoning laws have to be changed, and no consultants with expertise in things like traffic flow or signage have to be brought in.

That it has been well documented that older employees are an economic asset to any company rather than a liability is almost beside the point given the broader rationale for an age-friendly workplace. Besides making financial sense and demonstrating a genuine commitment to diversity and inclusion, an intergenerational workforce would actually go a long way toward ending ageism in everyday life. In his research, Karl Pillemer, the Cornell professor, has found that when you put people together from different generations, overall bias subsides; this carryover effect is yet another reason why it is so important that Big Business recognize its key role in ending ageism in America.

At some level, I can understand why Big Business is reluctant to invite older adults to their party. There is a large talent pool of younger adults from which to draw, after all, and many of them need money to pay off their college debt. They wear nice clothes, are well-groomed, and generally conform to our standards of beauty. Younger people tend to walk fast and look busy, in a hurry to get things done so that they can get more things done. As "digital natives," they understand technology and know how to use social media effectively. More broadly, we have always been considered a young country compared to most of those in Europe and Asia, so it makes sense that organizations would embrace youthfulness in the workplace.

This is all well and good save for the fact that it is highly discriminatory. Any and all forms of segregation shouldn't be tolerated, meaning we can't accept the redlining of Big Business even given the impressive attributes of 20- and 30-somethings. Whether millennials and members of Gen Z like it or not, there are tens of millions of 50-, 60-, and 70-somethings still very much around, and they too deserve to work to pay their bills. It may be difficult to believe, but a job provides just as much meaning for a 65-year-old as for a 25-year-old, another valid reason why ageism in the workplace is a terrible thing that has to be stopped. That baby boomers have chosen to not retire in great numbers should be a welcome development rather than how it has been received. Continuing to contribute to the tax base and delaying and likely decreasing Social Security benefits are just a couple of reasons why we should be happy about the prospect of more people willing and able to work.

It may seem trivial compared with the inequities of the workplace, but companies' failure to treat older consumers as equals is a contributing factor of cultural ageism. Just as Big Business wants nothing to do with older employees, so does it want nothing to do with older consumers. The same sort of stereotypes—older people are fragile, feeble, and frail—apply in both the earning and spending of money. While they serve nicely as comic foils in advertising and fully deserve targeting by marketers selling products and services specially designed for seniors—safer bathtubs, easy to use cellphones, prescription drugs, and memory pills, say—older people are otherwise considered not worth the expense to go after. This exclusion is a natural and logical extension of the marginalizing of older people in the workplace and in CSR. That the market is large and collectively wealthy—far more than millennials—makes the whole thing even stranger. All the statistics in the world can support the basis for the longevity economy but are considered almost meaningless due to marketers' myopia and obsession with coolness.

If diversity and inclusion initiatives are not enough to stop ageism in the workplace and marketplace despite being exactly what they are intended to be, perhaps Big Business's rush to be socially responsible is. If nothing else, CSR proves that Corporate America can change if it wants to, good news for making ageism just another part of its long history of discrimination. Age equality or neutrality is being socially responsible, it needs to be said, making what is currently taking place in the world of business socially irresponsible. As more companies and investors gravitate toward ESG, B corporation status, and other avenues of CSR, it will hopefully become more apparent that ageist thinking and practices do not at all fit into the model. Why be externally socially responsible but not internally? C-suite execs might ask this of themselves, perhaps then seeing the contradictions between doing good outside the company but failing to do so inside.

Adopting social responsibility as a philosophy or way of thinking versus just taking on a particular cause offers our greatest chance of ending ageism. The responsibility revolution is extremely flexible, after all, entirely accommodating of all kinds of business practices grounded in the idea of improving the world in some way. Making sustainability a company mantra is a means to forge a strategic vision and mission that reflects how the organization acts toward both employees and the general public. I would think it is easy to see the parallels between internal and external "greenness," but Corporate America appears to be cherry-picking which battles they want to fight. Only by exerting economic pressure on companies will the business community take action in the area, I believe, thus the reason why baby boomers have to express their voices through their dollars. Tell companies that have demonstrated age discrimination that you will no longer buy their product or service until they change their ways. As consumers, we have many choices, a form of power that has proven to be remarkably effective.

While Big Business can and should do whatever it can to end ageism, the larger opportunity resides in society as a whole. Finding ways to put people of different ages (and all other social divisions) together offers great potential in weakening the myths and stereotypes that form the backbone of ageism. Case studies in which bridges have been built between people of different ages have demonstrated the effectiveness of this, meaning we should actively encourage greater intergenerational mingling in both our personal and professional lives. People of different genders and skin tones often mix freely in our society, but many older people are siloed from younger people (in part because the former are not welcome in the workplace). A kind of cultural exchange program like the one in which people from different countries switch places for a year may not be a bad idea. Such a thing might bring out the often-forgotten truth that we are all more alike than different. Despite what the media tells us because bad news makes good news, we share many of the same values and want the same things out of life. Normalizing the aging process would go a long way to making this more apparent.

Encouraging local, state, and federal elected officials to create and enforce age bias laws would also be of great help. The government's failure to treat ageism equally to other forms of discrimination has served as a major contributor to the problem. History clearly shows that, despite their interest in social responsibility, companies often need to be pushed with regard to hiring practices. Large corporations are resistant to change, making something like age equality akin to turning the proverbial large ship around in the ocean. Many simply won't voluntarily open their doors to older workers, making it necessary to frame age discrimination within equal opportunity and civil rights laws. The U.S. Department of Labor is quite interested in this area, so put your tax money to work by informing the agency (or your state AARP rep) of potential violations. Letting your congressperson, state senator, U.S. senator, and governor know your thoughts about ageism and urging her or him to take appropriate action is also a good idea. Older people tend to vote in great numbers, making them a key constituency for any politician to seek at election time, an asset that should be fully leveraged.

Let's all work together to make our country and world age friendly for ourselves and for future generations.

Note

1 I am not the first to propose such a theory based in a kind of repulsion of one's future self. In a 1972 article in *The Gerontologist*, J. H. Bunzel coined the term "gerontophobia," defining it as "the unreasonable fear and/or hatred of the elderly" (J. H. Bunzel, "Note on the History of a Concept—Gerontophobia," *The Gerontologist* (1972), 12(2)). And in their book *Ageism: Prejudice and Discrimination Against the Elderly* in 1980, Jack Levin and William C. Levin expanded the concept a bit. "Gerontophobia seems to occur, first of all, because most young people will someday be old, and secondly, because old age is associated with death" (Levin, Jack, and William C. Levin, *Ageism: Prejudice and Discrimination Against the Elderly*. Belmont, CA: Wadsworth, 1980, p. 94).

Bibliography

Applewhite, Ashton. *This Chair Rocks: A Manifesto Against Ageism*. New York: Celadon Books, 2020.

Aronson, Louise. *Elderhood: Redefining Aging, Transforming Medicine, Reimagining Life*. New York: Bloomsbury, 2021.

Ayalon, Liat, and Clemens Tesch-Romer, eds. *Contemporary Perspectives on Ageism*. New York: Springer, 2018.

Barnes, Patricia G. *Betrayed: The Legalization of Age Discrimination in the Workplace*. Tucson: Patricia G. Barnes, 2014.

———. *Overcoming Age Discrimination in Employment: An Essential Guide for Workers, Advocates & Employers*. Tucson: Patricia G. Barnes, 2016.

Bazerman, Max H. *Better, Not Perfect: A Realist's Guide to Maximum Sustainable Goodness*. New York: Harper Business, 2020.

Billette, Veronique, Patrik Marier, and Anne-Marie Seguin, eds. *Getting Wise about Getting Old: Debunking Myths about Aging*. Vancouver, CA: University of British Columbia Press, 2020.

Blair, Margaret M. *Ownership and Control: Rethinking Corporate Governance for the Twenty-First Century*. Washington, DC: Brookings Institute Press, 1995.

Buffel, Tine, Sophie Handler, and Chris Phillipson, eds. *Age-Friendly Cities and Communities: A Global Perspective*. Bristol, UK: Policy, 2019.

Butler, Robert N., MD. *Why Survive? Being Old in America*. New York: Harper & Row, 1975.

———. *The Longevity Revolution: The Benefits and Challenges of Living a Long Life*. New York: Public Affairs, 2008.

Chudacoff, Howard. *How Old Are You? Age Consciousness in America*. Princeton, NJ: Princeton University Press, 1989.

Conley, Chip. *Wisdom at Work: The Making of a Modern Elder*. New York: Currency, 2018.

Coughlin, Joseph F. *The Longevity Economy: Unlocking the World's Fastest-Growing, Most Misunderstood Market*. New York: Public Affairs, 2017.

Cruikshank, Margaret. *Learning to Be Old: Gender, Culture, and Aging.* Lanham, MD: Rowman & Littlefield, 2013.

Dannenberg, Andrew L., Howard Frumkin, and Richard Jackson, eds. *Making Healthy Places: Designing and Building for Health, Well-Being, and Sustainability.* Washington, DC: Island Press, 2011.

Dychtwald, Ken, and Dan Kadlec. *A New Purpose: Redefining Money, Family, Work, Retirement, and Success.* New York: William Morrow, 2010.

Dychtwald, Ken, and Robert Morison. *What Retirees Want: A Holistic View of Life's Third Age.* Hoboken, NJ: Wiley, 2020.

Feldmann, Derrick, and Michael Alberg-Seberich. *The Corporate Social Mind: How Companies Lead Social Change from the Inside Out.* New York: Fast Company Press, 2020.

Fideler, Elizabeth. *Aging, Work, ad Retirement.* Lanham, MD: Rowman and Littlefield, 2020.

———, ed. *The Rowman and Littlefield Handbook on Aging and Work.* Lanham, MD: Rowman and Littlefield, 2021.

Gibney, Bruce. *A Generation of Sociopaths: How the Baby Boomers Betrayed America.* New York: Hachette, 2017.

Gullette, Margaret Morganroth. *Agewise: Fighting the New Ageism in America.* Chicago: University of Chicago Press, 2011.

Hubbell, Peter. *The Old Rush: Marketing for Gold in the Age of Aging.* Greenwich, CT: LID Publishing, 2014.

———. *Getting Better with Age: Improving Marketing in the Age of Aging.* Greenwich, CT: LID Publishing, 2015.

Irving, Paul. *The Upside of Aging: How Long Life Is Changing the World of Health, Work, Innovation, Policy and Purpose.* Hoboken, NJ: Wiley, 2014.

Jenkins, Jo Ann. *Disrupt Aging: A Bold New Path to Living Your Best Life at Every Age.* New York: Public Affairs, 2018.

Karpf, Anne. *How to Age.* New York: Picador, 2015.

Kurzweil, Ray, and Terry Grossman, MD. *Fantastic Voyage: Live Long Enough to Live Forever.* Emmaus, PA: Rodale Books, 2004.

Levin, Jack, and William C. Levin. *Ageism: Prejudice and Discrimination Against the Elderly.* Belmont, CA: Wadsworth, 1980.

Lustbader, Wendy. *Life Gets Better: The Unexpected Pleasures of Growing Older.* New York: TarcherPerigee, 2011.

Nelson, Todd D, ed. *Ageism: Stereotyping and Prejudice Against Older Persons.* Cambridge, MA: MIT Press, 2002.

Rocks, Patti Temple. *I'm Not Done: It's Time to Talk About Ageism in the Workplace.* Austin, TX: Lioncrest Publishing, 2019.

Samuel, Lawrence R. *Aging in America: A Cultural History.* Philadelphia: University of Pennsylvania Press, 2017a.

————. *Boomers 3.0: Marketing to Baby Boomers in Their Third Act of Life*. Santa Barbara, CA: Praeger, 2017b.

Schurman, Bradley. *The Super Age*. New York: HarperBusiness, 2022.

Sinclair, David, Ph.D. *Lifespan: Why We Age and Why We Don't Have To*. New York: Artia Books, 2019.

Stafford, Philip B., ed. *The Global Age-Friendly Community Movement: A Critical Appraisal*. New York: Berghahn Books, 2018.

Steel, Richard. *Elevated Economics: How Conscious Consumers Will Fuel the Future of Business*. New York: Fast Company Press, 2020.

Taylor, Lisa, and Fern Lebo. *The Talent Revolution: Longevity and the Future of Work*. Toronto, CA: Rotman-UTP Publishing, 2019.

Index

A

AARP, 7, 31–32, 42, 43, 52–53, 91, 130
  advocacy of legal rights of older adults, 115
  Age-Friendly Network, 40–41, 47–48
  collaborations of, 49
  #DisruptAging campaign, 84
  group efforts, 50
  Growing with Age platform, 116
  Livability Index, 47
  Living, Learning & Earning Longer
    (LL&EL), 8, 67–70, 73, 116
  "Longevity Economy Outlook,
    The" 85
  Second Career section, 65
AARP Foundation, 115, 116
Acknowledge-Grow-Embrace (AGE) frame-
    work, 121–122
active senior living, 46
Administration on Aging, 36
AdvantAge Initiative, 36
advertising, 83–84, 92–94
Age Discrimination in Employment Act
    (ADEA), 18, 30–31, 58, 66
Age Equity Alliance (AEA), 75–76
age friendliness, 3, 4, 8, 41, 45–46, 130
age-friendly communities, 35–36, 115,
    130–131
  and access, 49
  AdvantAge Initiative, 36
  Age-Friendly Network, AARP, 40–41,
    47–48
  boosterism, 51
  collaboration of public and private
    sectors, 42
  cross-pollination, 43–44
  and demographic shifts, 48
  and economic incentives, 48–49
  economies of scope, 43
  and federal government, 53–54
  group efforts, 50
  and intergenerationality, 44–45
  livability and built environment, 47
  Miami-Dade County Age- Friendly
    Initiative, 41, 44
  migration to hipster neighborhoods, 46
  migration to small towns, 46–457
  New Jersey, 53
  New York State, 53
  planning, 40
  and poverty, 39
  and public sector, 115
  and rejection of retirement, 39
  senior centers, 49–50
  silver tsunami, 36–39
  small rural towns, 42–43
  and suburbs, 38
  swapping of success stories, 51–52
  transportation, 51
  and unique characteristics of
    community, 43
  urban planners, 50–51
  and walkability, 45
Age-Friendly Communities Act, 53–54
Age Friendly Foundation, 74
Age-Friendly Health Systems initiative, 26–27
ageism, 1–3, 6, 11–12, 26, 127–128
  activism to combat, 18, 119, 130
  in advertising, 83
  contribution of researchers, 13, 14
  and courts, 29, 30
  everyday ageism, 27, 28

in health-care system, 27
hyper-ageism, 24
and lack of contact between
        generations, 44
"ok boomer" mini-movement, 27–28
origins of, 12–13
practices, impact on health, 20–21
reconstruction of image of old age, 14
youth-oriented culture, 15–18
age-positive score, 120
aging, 5, 6–7, 15, 16
    aging in place, 36, 38, 39, 42, 89
    biological phenomenon *vs.* social meanings
        of age, 12
    and cosmetics industry, 18, 93
    as a disease, 19–20
    movement, signs of, 129
    negative view of, 14
    as a privilege, 20
    process, 16
    stereotypes, 14, 15, 27, 116, 121, 132
Allure, 20, 93
Americans with Disabilities Act, 82
anti-aging, 2, 6, 14–15, 18–20, 93
Apple, 95
Army Sustainment Command (ASC), 122
assisted living facilities, 39, 91

B

baby boomers, 2, 3, 5, 6, 7, 37, 45–46
    achievements, 25
    bucket lists of, 96
    combat against ageism, 26
    communication of marketers
        with, 83
    and community, 98–99
    conspicuous consumption of, 25
    creativity, 97
    criticism towards, 23–25
    encore careers, 64–66
    entrepreneurship, 72
    generational traits of, 23
    gradual sidelining in workforce, 59
    and Gray Power, 99
    and health, 25
    and higher ground, 96–97
    and knowledge transfer, 70–72
    learning by, 96
    legacy formation, 99–100

market, 80
migration to hipster neighborhoods, 46
migration to small towns, 46–47
"ok boomer" mini-movement, 27–28
paying it forward, 99
purchasing power of, 82, 85, 93
rebooting, 96–97
rejection of retirement, 39, 82, 132
and transfer of wealth, 85–86
unretirement, 62–64
use of social media, 93–94
and youthfulness, 96
Bank of America, 87, 113
beauty industry, 14–15, 18–19, 20
Ben & Jerry's, 106
birthday cards, 21
B Lab, 106
BlackRock, 111
Botox, 20
brand switching, 94
bucket lists, 96

C

capitalism, 103, 106, 107, 109
Centers for Disease Control and
        Prevention, 36
Certified Age-Friendly Employer (CAFE)
        classification, 74
Changing the Narrative initiative, 74
Cisco, 113
Civil Rights Act of 1964, 58
Cleveland Institute of Music, 28
clinical research, ageism in, 27
cognitive functioning, 18, 21–22, 60
college towns, 46–47
commercials, 83–84, 95
Commission on Aging and Retirement
        Education (CARE), 38–39
Common Impact, 112
communal living, 90
Communication Workers of America, 29–30
connected economy, 112, 113
conspicuous consumption, 25
consultants in workplace, 75–76
Convention on the Rights of Older
        Persons, 129
corporate citizenship, 104, 108
corporate goodness programs, 113
corporate philanthropy, 107

corporate social responsibility (CSR), 8, 103–104,
132–133; *see also* workplace
Acknowledge-Grow-Embrace (AGE)
framework, 121–122
and competitive edge, 109–110
and COVID-19 pandemic, 106–107
employee activism, 119–120
and employment brand, 113
and ESG, 105, 110–111, 120
greening of organizations, 108
and investors, 110–111, 120
and leaders, 108, 121
and older workers, 114–118
performance with purpose approach, 106
and power of customers, 109
reasons to adopt, 105
Rocket Mortgage, 111–112
skills-based volunteer program, 112
sustainability, 106, 107, 108, 110
tactics, 112
volunteerism, 112, 113–114
cosmetics industry, 18, 93
COVID-19 pandemic, 41, 52, 93, 94,
106–107
creativity, 22, 97
cultural exchange programs, 133

D

Decade of Healthy Ageing, 26
Deloitte, 114
digital natives, 29, 132
#DisruptAging campaign, 84
diversity and inclusion (D&I) initiative, 61,
74–75, 117, 120, 122, 131

E

economies of scope, 43
Economist Intelligence Unit, 31, 85
economy, 22, 23, 25
connected economy, 112, 113
impact of workplace ageism on, 31, 117
longevity economy, 8, 84–85, 87, 88, 132
and multigenerational workforce, 69
silver economy, 84, 86
elder care, 86
employee activism, 119–120
employment brand, 113
empty nesters, 45, 90, 98

encore careers, 64–66
Encore.org, 65
entrepreneurship, 72
Equal Employment Opportunity
Commission, 121
ESG (environmental, social, and governance),
105, 110–111, 120
experieneurship, 72

F

Facebook, 93–94
falls in older adults, 51–52
Fast Company, 105
Forbes Media, 73–74
forced retirement, 17

G

General Motors, 71
Generation X, 23, 24, 71
Generation Y, *see* millennials
Generation Z, 24, 27, 76, 129–130
geriatric medicine, 18
gerontology, 17, 18
Global Coalition on Aging (GCOA), 86–87
Global Institute for Experienced Entrepreneurship
(GIEE), 72
Global Network for Age-friendly Cities and
Communities, WHO, 7, 40
Grantmakers in Aging, 36
Gray Panthers, 18
Greatest Generation, 2
Great Society programs, 18, 107
Gross v. FBL Financial Services, 29
Growing with Age platform, 116

H

health, 25, 86
Age-Friendly Health Systems
initiative, 26–27
brain health, 21
problems, and ageism, 20–21, 28
and senior centers, 50
telehealth, 89
Health Across All Policies initiative, 53
health care, 6, 25, 26–27
hipster neighborhoods, migration of older
people to, 46

hiring practices, 29, 30, 58, 67, 68, 83, 119
Hollywood, 15
Home Instead Senior Care, 95
hyper-ageism, 24

I

IBM, 30
impact investing, 104, 120
inclusion nudges, 83
Institute for Healthcare Improvement, 26
intellectual capital, 70–72
intergenerational centers, 44
intergenerationality, 44–45, 46–47, 90, 133
intergenerational learning, 28–29
International City-County Management
Association, 49
investors, and CSR, 110–111, 120
invisible hand, 107

J

job shadowing, 71
John A. Hartford Foundation, 26

K

knowledge transfer, 70–72, 73

L

learning capability of baby boomers, 96
life expectancy, 4, 72, 85
LinkedIn, 117
Livability Index, AARP, 47
Living, Learning & Earning Longer (LL&EL),
8, 67–70, 73, 116
longevity economy, 8, 84–85, 87, 88

M

marketing, age-friendly, 8, 79–80, 132
advertising, 83–84, 92–94
aging as an opportunity, 82, 86–88
and aging in place, 89
brand switching, 94
cosmetics industry, 93
#DisruptAging campaign, 84
and experience of older adults, 92–93
Facebook, 93–94

Global Coalition on Aging, 86–87
longevity economy, 84–85, 87, 88
older consumers *vs.* younger
consumers, 84
oldness as a social construct, 81
prescription medications, 92
products designed for older people, 89
and retirement, 82–83
smart pills, 92
social design, 90
strategies, 95–100
and transfer of wealth, 85–86
wealth of baby boomers, 85
Masonicare-Quinnipiac University Students in
Residence Program, 28
MediaVillage, 74
Medicaid, 18, 39
medical marijuana, 79
Medicare, 2, 18, 62
mental health, 21, 49
mentoring, 73, 122
Miami-Dade County Age- Friendly Initiative,
41, 44
millennials, 7, 23, 24, 25, 59, 71, 111
Mind&Melody program, 44
mini-grants, 41, 44
mixed-income developments, 45
Modern Elder Academy (MEA), 60
modern elderhood, 59
multigenerational workforce, 63, 67, 68–69,
116, 117, 121

N

National Association of Area Agencies on
Aging, 36
National Employment Lawyers Association,
115
National Poll on Healthy Aging, 28
new urbanism, 45, 49
NextFifty Initiative, 74

O

"ok boomer" mini-movement, 27–28
old age homes, 17
Older Americans Act of 1965, 18, 35, 54
online shopping, 94
Organisation for Economic Co-operation and
Development (OECD), 8, 67, 68

organizational culture, and inclusivity, 68
overqualification, 7, 60

P

Patagonia, 106
pensions, 17
performance-and-image enhancing drugs
    (PIED), 92
performance with purpose approach, 106
phased retirement, 73
pickleball, 95
Place for Mom, A (APFM), 91
popular culture, 21
poverty, 39
prescription medications, 92
Primetime Partners, 88
productive aging, 5
productivity, and multigenerational
    workforce, 69
Protecting Older Workers Against
    Discrimination Act (POWADA),
    31–32
purchasing power of baby boomers, 82,
    85, 93

Q

Quinnipiac University, 28

R

retirement, 17, 39, 72–73; *see also* age-friendly
    communities
  forced, 17
  gap, 64
  and marketing, 82–83
  phased, 73
  savings, 64
  unretirement, 62–64
reverse mentoring, 122
Rocket Mortgage, 111–112
rural towns, age-friendly communities in,
    42–43

S

Salesforce, 114
Sand Buckets for Seniors program, 52
senior care workers, 82

senior centers, 49–50
senior cohousing communities (SCCs), 90
sexuality of older people, 22
Shiseido, 93
Shorewood Connects, 50
Silver Disobedience, 87–88
silver economy, 84, 86
Silvernest, 90
silver tsunami, 3, 36–39
smart homes, 89
smart pills, 92
social design, 90
social engagement/interaction, 40, 49, 50
social isolation, 51, 52
social media, 93–94, 109, 132
social network, 98–99
Social Security, 2, 17, 39, 62, 63
Social Security Act of 1935, 17
Stanford Center on Longevity (SCOL), 87
Starbucks, 110
stereotypes, ageist, 14, 15, 27, 116, 121, 132
suburbs
  demographic makeup of, 38
  migration to urban areas from, 45, 46
successful aging, 5
Supreme Court, 29, 66
sustainability, 106, 107, 108, 110, 133

T

tech industry, 30, 58, 123
technology, 22, 44–45, 132
telehealth, 89
thought leadership, 86
Timberland, 113
transportation, 51
TripAdvisor, 114

U

United Nations (UN), 40, 129
unretirement, 62–64
urban planners, 50–51
U.S. Department of Labor, 134

V

venture capitalists, 82, 88
volunteering, 43, 50, 52, 100, 112,
    113–114

W

walkability, neighborhood, 45
walking audits, 50
What's Next Longevity Summit, 88
woke capitalism, 106, 109
women, 20, 85–86
workplace, 57–58, 131–132
  Acknowledge-Grow-Embrace (AGE)
    framework, 121–122
  "Act Deterring Age Discrimination in
    Employment Application, An,"
    Connecticut, 117–118
  Age Discrimination in Employment Act,
    18, 30–31, 58, 66
  ageism in, 7–8, 15, 29, 31, 57–58, 58–59,
    60–61, 66, 117
  age-neutral workplace, 122
  Bill A-681, New Jersey, 118
  consultants in, 75–76
  diversity and inclusion initiative, 61,
    74–75, 117, 120, 122, 131
  employee activism, 119–120
  encore careers, 64–66
  flexibilities in, 65, 68
  hiring practices, 29, 30, 58, 67, 68, 119
  and knowledge transfer, 70–72, 73
  and legal actions, 120–121
  legislation to end age discrimination,
    117–118
  Living, Learning & Earning Longer
    (LL&EL), 8, 67–70, 73, 116
  modern elderhood, 59
  multigenerational workforce, 63, 67,
    68–69, 116, 117, 121
  myths about older people, 60–61, 117
  older consumers and older workers, 69
  overqualification, 7, 60
  Protecting Older Workers Against
    Discrimination Act, 31–32
  and retirement, 72–73
  rights of older workers, 29–30, 115–116
  small businesses, 60
  social contract between employers and
    employees, 73
  and unretirement, 62–64
World Economic Forum (WEF), 8, 67, 68
World Health Organization (WHO), 7, 26,
  40, 45

Y

YMCA, 49
youth-oriented culture, 11, 15–18

Printed in the United States
by Baker & Taylor Publisher Services